HAY HOUSE BASICS

SELF-HYPNOSIS

❖ Also in the Hay House Basics series ❖

Crystals

Mindfulness

Past Lives

Angels

Lucid Dreaming

Tarot

Energy Healing

NLP

Coming soon

Reiki

Numerology

Feng Shui

Shamanism

Astrology

SELF-HYPNOSIS

Reach Your Full Potential Using All of Your Mind

VALERIE AUSTIN

HAY
HOUSE

HAY HOUSE

Carlsbad, California • New York City • London • Sydney
Johannesburg • Vancouver • Hong Kong • New Delhi

First published and distributed in the United Kingdom by:
Hay House UK Ltd, Astley House, 33 Notting Hill Gate, London W11 3JQ
Tel: +44 (0)20 3675 2450; Fax: +44 (0)20 3675 2451
www.hayhouse.co.uk

Published and distributed in the United States of America by:
Hay House Inc., PO Box 5100, Carlsbad, CA 92018-5100
Tel: (1) 760 431 7695 or (800) 654 5126; Fax: (1) 760 431 6948 or (800) 650 5115
www.hayhouse.com

Published and distributed in Australia by:
Hay House Australia Ltd, 18/36 Ralph St, Alexandria NSW 2015
Tel: (61) 2 9669 4299; Fax: (61) 2 9669 4144; www.hayhouse.com.au

Published and distributed in the Republic of South Africa by:
Hay House SA (Pty) Ltd, PO Box 990, Witkoppen 2068
info@hayhouse.co.za; www.hayhouse.co.za

Published and distributed in India by:
Hay House Publishers India, Muskaan Complex, Plot No.3, B-2,
Vasant Kunj, New Delhi 110 070
Tel: (91) 11 4176 1620; Fax: (91) 11 4176 1630; www.hayhouse.co.in

Distributed in Canada by:
Raincoast Books, 2440 Viking Way, Richmond, B.C. V6V 1N2
Tel: (1) 604 448 7100; Fax: (1) 604 270 7161; www.raincoast.com

A catalogue record for this book is available from the British Library.

ISBN: 978-1-78180-499-5

Interior illustations © graphicsdunia4you/thinkstockphotos.co.uk

To my husband, James – a biographer and researcher whose knowledge of hypnosis is second to none.

Contents

Acknowledgements

I owe a special debt of thanks to the people of Langkawi, where I wrote my first self-hypnosis book and was able to develop so many of my techniques working with fascinating people from so many different cultures.

Some special hypnotists have inspired me throughout my career. John Watkins PhD for making available to me his film on his excellent work on regression to treat war trauma and his advice. Dr Jack Gibson, a surgeon and pioneer in painless surgery with hypnosis. Ormond McGill, who put a gentlemanly excitement and fun into hypnosis. Jerry Valley, with whom I learned the art of stage hypnosis, which gave me more understanding on how the mind works. Gil Boyne, who helped me regain a big part of my memory after my car accident and who was instrumental in my early training. Reg Morton for his help in my legal matters through the years and also Mike Payne for his patience with my technical issues.

Don Green, CEO of the Napoleon Hill Foundation, who gave me his special insights on Napoleon Hill. A special thanks to Inger Garcia, my attorney, co-producer of our films and documentaries and friend; her diagnosis of stage four breast cancer was instrumental in furthering my understanding of the importance of self-hypnosis for cancer sufferers and their families. Sally Farmiloe, a friend since her *Howards' Way* days: a very brave and intelligent lady who fought bravely against the aggressive cancer before she so tragically died.

There are many other people to thank for their help over the years. Kevin James for his help and invaluable contributions. Dr O'Brook, an excellent psychiatrist who recommended many clients to me in my early days in Harley Street. Dr Alan Sanderson, psychiatrist and hypnotherapist, who has always been available for advice. Pierre Marcar and Katie Glen and the many students for their input in researching therapies and scripts that have proved to be exceedingly successful.

Dr Abdul Halim Othman, Dean at the University Kebangsaan (UKM), Malaysia who invited me to teach my 7-day Advanced Hypnotherapy course to a selection of professors and students at this leading University of Psychology. This resulted in the Health Minister of Malaysia formally giving his approval for the Austin 'Stop Smoking in One Hour' technique. Another of my former Malaysian students, Julian Leicester, is now following in my footsteps and winning prestigious awards for his work in stopping smoking using hypnosis. To the many friends I made while I was working there.

Special thanks to Hay House for giving me the opportunity to share my knowledge with everyone and to my editor Amy whose enthusiasm for the project has encouraged and helped me every step of the way.

Finally, I'm indebted to the thousands of clients and many hundreds of therapists I've trained for helping to further educate me in the extraordinary workings of the mind and how easily it can be changed.

Introduction

From Hollywood to hypnotherapy

Self-hypnosis can be used to stop smoking, eliminate phobias, reduce your weight, help you sleep, reduce stress, enjoy relationships, maximize your potential and more – in fact the list is endless. And to make these changes it only takes the use of specific words in a hypnotic trance. It sounds so easy and it really is.

What's more, overcoming a 'major' problem can create a snowball effect because in clearing away one issue you will find many other difficulties, connected with the major issue, begin to evaporate too. For example, you might use self-hypnosis to help you lose weight or get fitter and, as it begins to work, so your self-confidence and self-esteem increase too. Think of it as a mind clean up to start the process of creating the life you want. But self-hypnosis doesn't only have to be used for problems but can also be used to make life easier for you, for example, to give you more confidence in yourself, allow you to enjoy life more, enhance your sports, music, art ability or even help you to learn a language or other skill more rapidly.

However, before you start reading how to use self-hypnosis to create these and more incredible outcomes in your life, you may be wondering why I am able to teach you how to get the most out of hypnotizing yourself. It's partly due to my extensive research and 30 years' experience of practising and teaching hypnotherapy, but, mainly it's owing to the memory loss I suffered in a near-fatal car accident in 1978, which eventually inspired me to switch roles from Hollywood reporter and magazine publisher to hypnotherapist.

After the accident I suffered amnesia, leaving me with a 24-hour memory. When the *Daily Mirror* heard about this strange phenomenon, they featured me in an article entitled 'Will Bride Remember Her Husband?'. While holidaying in California, John Austin (international editor of *The Hollywood Reporter*) had proposed to me. The problem? I was in danger of forgetting he even existed when I returned to the UK.

A well-known hypnotherapist from the USA (Gil Boyne) was visiting London at the time and contacted me after reading the article. Under hypnosis, he was able to help me regain part of my memory and literally give me back my life. From then on I took a keen interest in understanding the complexity and workings of the inner mind which has given me a unique perspective on the subject of hypnosis.

Living in the 'NOW'

When I first had the accident, I could only remember one day at a time and only a little of the past if I were asked about it; otherwise, I lived in the 'now'. Not being able to remember properly, I found I functioned in the almost 'pure' subconscious. As a result, when I was commissioned to teach my hypnotherapy course in universities I didn't even make notes, as I simply wouldn't have remembered that I had made them. This left me with no alternative but to work purely from my subconscious.

However, this unique understanding of the workings of the subconscious mind gave me a special edge when working with clients to resolve their issues, and this was paramount to becoming a successful hypnotherapist. I was able to come up with successful, new and innovative hypnosis techniques that were easily taught because of their simplicity. These new methods have now helped many people over the years to make positive, and sometimes life-saving, changes.

As well as having extensively studied and taught hypnotherapy and self-hypnosis to other therapists and clients, I've always maintained that the secret of good results from hypnotherapy is the ability to use self-hypnosis outside the consulting room. I've tested my self-hypnosis scripts with hypnotherapists I've trained and with clients, so I know how effective they are.

In recent years, I've been able to help two close friends use self-hypnosis to help them through their ordeal of dealing with a cancer diagnosis. The power of the mind has been acknowledged as a contributory factor in pain relief and aiding recovery from serious illnesses, and they both acknowledge that a daily dose of self-hypnosis made a huge difference to them.

As well as having trained hundreds of therapists for three decades, I've worked with thousands of clients, and written five bestselling books, which were translated into six languages. I believe the three most important reasons why I was able to become a top hypnotherapist were my background: first, before my car accident I was always one of the top salespeople in my company. Second, I was an investigative reporter for major newspapers before also publishing two of my own major London magazines, *London People* and *Weekend People*. Finally, and most importantly, I was trained by some of the most influential hypnotherapists, including Gil Boyne, surgeon Dr Jack Gibson and Ormond McGill. Psychologist John G Watkins was a friend of my husband and was a great help in explaining the therapeutic strategies that became the basis of my technique for recovering traumatic memories.

In this book you will find techniques and self-hypnosis scripts for changing and improving your life, as well as dealing with issues such as phobias and weight loss, together with case studies from my own practice and those of hypnotherapists I've trained over the years. I look forward to sharing this knowledge and experience with you, showing you just how powerful self-hypnosis can be.

Hyp-notes

Throughout the book, I use a few terms that have special meanings in the language of hypnosis, so I have included them below.

Depth of trance: The words used to describe the level of hypnosis.

Deepeners: The words used to deepen a trance.

Hypnotist: Someone who practices hypnosis. Hypnotherapist is a relatively new word but describes a hypnotist who uses therapy while his patient or client is in hypnosis.

Induction: The words used to 'induce' a hypnotic trance.

Relaxation: Being fully relaxed and breathing deeply and rhythmically. Deep relaxation sounds simple but it is generally something that has to be learned through practice, patience and persistence.

Subconscious: In hypnosis the subconscious or inner mind seems to be nearer the surface and is more readily accessible to suggestion.

Suggestibility: A person's susceptibility to accepting a suggestion in hypnosis.

Suggestions: The words used in hypnosis to instruct the subconscious mind to create change. Hippolyte Bernheim, a 19th-century French physician and one of the founders of modern hypnotherapy, explained that 'suggestion is an event through which an idea is introduced into the mind and accepted by it'.[1]

Script: This is the exact wording that is used to form a new program for the subconscious to follow.

Part I
UNDERSTANDING SELF-HYPNOSIS

'Imagination is the language of the subconscious and hypnosis is the key to the inner mind.'

Chapter 1

The history of hypnosis and self-hypnosis

'True wisdom comes to each of us when we realize how little we understand about life, ourselves, and the world around us.'

Socrates

The term 'self-hypnosis' is taken from the expression 'autosuggestion', coined in the early 1900s by a French pharmacist, Émile Coué, who was so amazed by the power of hypnosis that he wanted to teach others to cure their own illnesses without the aid of a hypnotist, and so self-hypnosis came into the public awareness for the first time. However, he worried about the term hypnosis so changed the name to autosuggestion, which we now know as self-hypnosis. Teaching his patients to use his short suggestions in trance resulted in powerful changes. It made such an impact that autosuggestion became the rage of Paris and later swept through the USA and the UK with staggeringly successful results.

So how important is self-hypnosis in our lives today? In the greatest book ever written on being successful, *Think and Grow Rich*, the author, Napoleon Hill, devotes an entire chapter to self-hypnosis. Some people have been able to use self-hypnosis naturally and become fabulously successful, as Hill discovered when he interviewed hundreds of people, including 50 of the top businessmen in the USA such as Andrew Carnegie and Henry Ford, to discover their secrets. The following chapters and exercises will teach you how to have the same pattern of thinking as the very successful – even if you're completely new to hypnosis. But before looking at the modern-day uses of self-hypnosis and learning how to use it in your own life, you may find it helpful to understand a little of the rich and colourful history of hypnosis and how it all began around 200 years ago.

From Mesmerism to hypnotism

In the beginning, and as a precursor to hypnosis, there was Franz Mesmer (1734–1815), a brilliant Viennese physician, who believed there was a magnetic force in the universe and created a method to harness this force for healing. He called it 'animal magnetism', which he discovered could be created by focusing intensely on his subject while passing his hands in front of their bodies. Such passes of hands were later called 'Mesmeric passes'. He was an extraordinary man with many interests including music, and he would later use the glass harmonica to induce trance states. He was a friend of the Mozart family and the young Wolfgang performed one of his concerts in Mesmer's garden theatre. His large gardens would eventually be used to cater for the huge crowds that wanted his healing.

It was an extraordinary time, when gravity, electricity, magnetism and chemical reactions were being discovered, while doctors had little to offer beyond potions, bleeding,and purges. Even worse, the most popular drug, calomel, contained mercury: a deadly poison that, when used regularly, caused the patient's teeth and hair to fall out and an early death. Mesmerism quickly grew in popularity and Mesmer treated thousands of patients before leaving Austria to go to Paris because of the hostility he faced from the medical establishment.

Arriving in Paris, Mesmerism quickly became all the rage but, again, it had doctors worried, as they were losing patients to this new phenomenon and there was talk of it possibly creating political instability. The result was an official Royal Investigation in 1784. The committee said that Mesmerism was most likely due to belief and imagination rather than an invisible energy. However, they begrudgingly admitted that patients treated with animal magnetism did get better.

Many hypnosis books claimed that Mesmer then disappeared a broken man, but that was far from the truth. The reality was that he made more money after the investigation and became extremely successful and fabulously wealthy.

As part of his work and research Mesmer experimented with making passes over parts of his own body, which was in effect the first self-Mesmerism, or an early form of self-hypnosis. However, this form of trance healing, which could be used on oneself, was then largely forgotten for almost 100 years.

Up until fairly recently, although Mesmerism was proven to work, it was Mesmer's beliefs about the energy force that were in question. Now, with new science and technology, it seems as though he was correct. One thing is for sure – Mesmerism was the first system of trance energy healing. It uses both energy work and suggestion whereas hypnosis relies only on suggestion.

Two doctors who became famous for practicing Mesmerism were James Esdaile (1808–59) and John Elliotson (1791–1868). James Esdaile was a Scottish surgeon and performed hundreds of surgeries whilst working in India using Mesmerism as the only form of anaesthesia. Some patients reported suffering no pain at all, even after the surgery and in the healing process. Esdaile discovered that his patients had lower mortality rates, fewer post-operative infections, reduced bleeding and faster recovery times.

John Elliotson was a professor of medicine at the University of London who started to teach doctors how to use Mesmerism for painless surgery and founded a number of hospitals throughout Britain and Ireland. He was heavily criticized by doctors, who even went so far as to say that they believed his patients were only pretending not to feel pain. In one instance, they even said a man was just pretending to have no pain as his leg was amputated – which would, of course, be impossible.

Other famous Mesmerists included authors Charles Dickens, who had been taught by Elliotson, and Alexandre Dumas, who wrote *The Count of Monte Cristo*.

The beginnings of hypnotism

James Braid (1795–1860), another Scottish doctor, having seen Mesmerism performed in Manchester, believed it was just 'visual fixation', so instead of Mesmeric passes he had his patients focus on a shiny object, such as a lit candle or a mirror to induce a trance. To describe this sleep-like state, he coined the word 'hypnosis' – derived from the Greek word *hypnos*, which means 'sleep'. With more research on his patients, however, he realized that hypnosis had very little to do with sleep, so he tried to popularize another, more accurate term, 'monoideism' – meaning a fixation of attention – but it never caught on.

Throughout the 19th century Mesmerism continued to be far more popular than hypnosis and gained more respectability when Jean-Martin Charcot (1825–93), a French physician considered to be the founder of modern neurology, presented his scientific findings on Mesmerism and hypnosis to the Academy of Sciences in 1882. Although some of Charcot's theories of how hypnosis worked were later proven to be incorrect, his important discovery relevant to self-hypnosis was that the 'hypnoid' state[2] (a state resembling sleep or hypnosis) could enable the patient to resolve their own conditions through autosuggestion.

> '*The Time will come when the Truth will be proven beyond a doubt, and humanity will thank me.*' – MESMER

During this time Hippolyte Bernheim (1840–1919), another French physician, became the most famous hypnotist of his generation by using hypnosis with his patients at the Nancy School in Alsace, France. Already renowned for his research on typhoid, Bernheim worked with 10,000 patients using hypnosis and argued that anyone could be hypnotized because it was an extension of normal psychological functioning. He said its effects were due to suggestion, saying, 'Suggestion is an idea that changes into action.'[3] After decades of debate, Bernheim's view dominated whilst Charcot's theory is now just a historical curiosity.

Sigmund Freud (1856–1939), the founder of modern psychoanalysis, spent four months with Charcot, who was conducting studies in hypnotism at Salpêtrière Hospital, and also studied with Bernheim at the Nancy School. Despite seeing how effective hypnosis was, and initially using it, he then abandoned it in favour of his newly developed 'psychoanalysis'. However, Freud's earlier writings reveal the rich history of hypnosis and acknowledged how much the theory of psychoanalysis was indebted to it. At one time Freud was so interested in hypnosis that he volunteered to translate Bernheim's book into German, showing his early commitment to it. Although Freud admitted he was not comfortable working with hypnosis, he never lost his fascination for it.

Self-hypnosis becomes the fashion

Émile Coué (1857–1926), a French pharmacist who studied chemistry in Paris, was called the founder of self-hypnosis and was the most successful advocate in its history. No one has ever measured up to his phenomenal achievements, not only in France but also in the USA and the UK. His message was simple and he taught thousands of people to 'think away your sickness'. As the proprietor of a pharmacy, Coué noticed that the suggestions he gave his customers when giving them their prescriptions had a positive effect on their recovery. What he said was very simple: he praised the medicine, told them to read the instructions on the prescription and that they would recover quickly. He began to realize that just their belief that the medicine would work hastened their recovery. He later gave up medicine altogether, choosing to focus on only using the mind for healing.

While Coué's aim was to help people heal themselves, he believed that the word 'hypnosis' gave the wrong impression and believed people might think they were being controlled, and be frightened by it. There were also problems from other medical doctors who still opposed hypnosis. So Coué began to develop a simple process to create a trance by using repetition and short direct suggestions. He found the term autosuggestion to be immediately accepted by the public and he no longer had to worry too much about negative feedback. As a result, Coué was by far the most successful advocate of self-hypnosis and the majority of modern self-help books refer to affirmations or some form of autosuggestion or self-hypnosis. However, whilst these utilize the 'conscious' mind to bring about changes through repetition, suggestions given directly to the 'subconscious' mind when in self-hypnosis are proven to be far more powerful, while also reducing the time taken to bring about changes.

We have the power to heal within ourselves
by using focused imagination and when
our imagination and our 'will' are opposed,
imagination is invariably the winner. Coué
called this 'The Law of Reversed Effort'.

Modern hypnosis and hypnotherapy

Milton Erickson MD (1901–80) is probably the best-known clinical hypnotherapist of the 20th century. Erickson worked as a psychiatrist in Michigan and an associate professor of psychiatry in Detroit, and wrote a number of brilliant scholarly articles on his research on clinical hypnosis early in his career. A significant part of his work was based on observational skills, which he developed during his years of illness in childhood when he suffered from polio. He carefully watched each subject and scrutinized facial expressions and slight body movements to tailor his hypnosis to each patient. For a number of years he travelled throughout the USA teaching hypnosis to doctors; however, later in life he was struck with a second attack of polio and from then on was severely infirm.

It was during this time that several collaborators, most notably Ernest Rossi, began to work with him. By now Erickson had been forced to change the way he hypnotized patients because of his illness. He was no longer the dynamic, energetic man he had been before. As a result, almost all of the books written about his work are classed more as indirect hypnosis than direct hypnosis. In attempting to analyse precisely how Erickson worked, his collaborators often became overly complex and got immersed in the minute details; this then gave birth to a field of study called 'Ericksonian hypnosis'. These volumes range in quality but few of them approach the brilliance of Erickson's early articles on his extraordinary research yet, unfortunately, these are rarely included or referenced in hypnosis training for modern-day hypnotherapists.

Indirect hypnosis is, of course, popular with some hypnotherapists because it seems fail-safe. Instead of giving a direct suggestion, the most extreme form of indirect suggestion would say, 'Your arm may go up, it may go down or it may do nothing at all'. This, of course, is not really suited to self-hypnosis. However, despite writing very little about self-hypnosis, due to focusing mainly on patient therapy, Erickson did recognize its potential.

Evidence in practice

Despite the long history of hypnosis, and proof that it works, the medical establishment's views have only improved a little and there is still a reluctance to acknowledge the effectiveness of hypnosis. Unfortunately it is often used as a 'last resort' instead of a first consideration or, at the very least, a complementary procedure to medical intervention, speeding the healing process and giving patients the enthusiasm to eat the correct foods and work on building their health.

It was only in 2002 that unquestionable 'scientific' proof of how hypnosis works made the headlines in the major newspapers, giving it another 15 minutes of fame before disappearing again. A research project using PET scans showed how a volunteer's blood flow changed direction on command from a hypnotist whilst the person was in trance. The pictures were indisputable evidence of the power of hypnosis.[4] Despite this type of story appearing once in a while, the press still claim there is no proof that it works.

However, there is evidence every day that it DOES work and has become more widely accepted, with dentists using hypnosis to stop bleeding, painless operations being carried out using hypnosis instead of anaesthetic, and paramedics using it to help people in shock and save lives. This is apart from its usual higher-profile uses, such as phobia cures, weight loss and smoking cessation, which seem to be more predominantly featured in the press, as they make more of an impact on readers. But there is no substitute for learning to hypnotize yourself and formulating your own suggestions, in much the same way as Coué did for health and Napoleon Hill for business. You can harness the incredible power of your mind for making changes in your life and this book will teach you how.

RECAP ✍

* Hypnosis has a 200-year history.

* Hypnosis has always been used in medicine, even for painless operations.

* Since the days of Mesmer, innovative physicians have been researching the medical uses of hypnosis.

* Autosuggestion is recognized as the precursor to modern-day self-hypnosis.

Chapter 2

The power of hypnosis

'Autosuggestion is the medium for influencing the subconscious mind.'

NAPOLEON HILL

There is no debate that hypnosis exists or works, as throughout its 200-year history, hypnosis and hypnotherapy have been proven by thousands of clinical cases and experiments that have been documented in books and journals.[5-6] However, science can't agree on 'how' or 'why' it works. We know that in a hypnotic trance the subject is not asleep but rather in an altered state, which can be induced by deep relaxation techniques or by confusion and/or shock tactics. In other words, deep relaxation does not equal a hypnotic state and you can be in what resembles a waking state (observed, for example, in stage hypnosis) and be in deep hypnotic trance. The main difference is that when you are in hypnosis the subconscious becomes accessible and is much more receptive to powerful suggestions for change. So when you induce a state of self-hypnosis, you are simply bringing about an altered state of consciousness. Like switching on a computer, the 'trance-state' allows you access to your subconscious.

You can't check to see if someone is in a hypnotic trance by measuring the depth of their relaxation alone. You need to test the person's responses to suggestions. As you can imagine, this is very confusing for scientific research and precisely why the experts came up with a series of tests to see what level of hypnosis you have reached, but it needs a hypnotherapist to check for signs.

In self-hypnosis you don't have an option to test the depth of your trance, so you have to depend on the results. It is a little like trying to test if a remark you have just heard works for you in a conversation, but you are alone so can't get any feedback – it's untestable. However, in Chapter 4 you'll find some techniques to help you improve the quality of your hypnosis. These include what are called 'deepeners' to help you go deeper into a hypnotic state. Using these suggestions, you can decide just how deep into hypnosis you want to go. They include the classic 'Ruler deepener' (*see pages 65–66*), which hypnotherapists use to deepen a client's trance. Using this technique on a regular basis would give you an idea of the depth of trance you are achieving.

Hyp-notes

People ask me if hypnosis is dangerous and this is a question born mainly out of not knowing what hypnosis actually is. Some people may have only seen a stage hypnosis show, a video on the Internet or hypnosis on TV, which could lead to a belief that you can be made to do things against your will or have no control in hypnosis. This is simply not the case and you are always in control, especially with self-hypnosis, where there is no hypnotist involved and only YOU take part in the process. Another myth is that you can get 'stuck' in hypnosis but again this isn't true, as you naturally emerge from this relaxed state if you don't count yourself out, just like waking up from being asleep. Some people may find they want to stay in hypnosis for a little longer voluntarily and enjoy the deep relaxation, and automatically come out of this state when they are ready.

I can safely say that I have never had any of these problems with my thousands of clients throughout my long career as a hypnotherapist and neither have the hundreds of hypnotherapists I have trained. Hypnosis is simply a form of relaxation with varying depths of trance, and so the effects can only be positive, both physically and psychologically.

In learning self-hypnosis, you will discover its amazing power for improving any aspects of your life, quickly and easily. Once you learn how to use the natural processes of self-talk and imagery, you'll realize that you are always in full control and can easily put yourself into a hypnotic state. This can be done by either listening to a recording or facilitating it via a series of techniques to relax your body and mind. This in turn allows you to access your subconscious. You can then use specially designed suggestions (as in hypnotherapy) to bring about powerful changes in your life. If you put into practice the information in this book and practise the techniques I recommend, you will quickly become skilled in the art of self-hypnosis and reap its untold benefits.

What can self-hypnosis treat?

Hypnosis is able to help with many ailments and problems, both psychological and physical. Most people know how hypnosis can help with issues such as weight loss, smoking cessation, lack of self-esteem and so on, but many physical illnesses can also be greatly helped with self-hypnosis because hypnosis allows the mind and body to relax immediately, giving it a surplus of energy to rest and heal itself. Specific suggestions can also be formulated to target symptoms or for pain management.

In many instances, hypnosis can also be used as an alternative or complementary therapy to traditional medication, alleviating the possibility of suffering the inevitable side effects of modern drugs.

Case study

A student on my Medical Hypnosis course had allergies and was frightened that the chemical anaesthesia would be too aggressive and cause complications in an operation she was due to have. Another student worked with her under the supervision of my husband James Pool, who was the instructor on the course. The result was that she had two successful operations using hypnosis without feeling any pain, despite the absence of any anaesthetic.

In addition, self-hypnosis can help maintain a healthy weight and lifestyle and so help you to avoid illnesses such as type 2 diabetes and heart disease. Other more minor physical ailments, such as warts, can also be resolved using hypnosis because, like other physical conditions, such as blushing and even IBS (irritable bowel syndrome), there can be a psychological component.

Perhaps most famously hypnotherapy has been hugely successful in helping people quit smoking. In fact a report in *New Scientist* in 1992 named it the most effective way of giving up smoking, while Von Dedenroth, a hypnotherapy researcher, published an article in the *American Journal of Clinical Hypnosis* in 1968 giving hypnosis a 94 per cent success rate in smoking cessation. My own 'Stop Smoking in One Hour' technique has a success rate of 95 per cent using similar techniques.

Hypnosis has also been clinically demonstrated to facilitate positive outcomes in changing behaviours, most notably, perhaps, weight loss, accelerated learning, stress management, acute pain relief and phobias.

Case study

This may explain why everything is not as it seems when dealing with phobias. Very often a fear or phobia can't be identified using conscious reasoning or memories. Hypnosis is the only way to establish the 'root' of the problem. For example, a colleague helped a young girl overcome her dreadful fear of cats. The fear was so extreme that if there was a cat in the same room she broke out into a rash and had panic attacks. In hypnosis the girl found that the first time she had a fear of a cat was when she was a baby asleep in her pram. A loud crack of thunder woke her and, at the same time, a cat, also frightened by the thunderclap, jumped over her pram. The crash of thunder and the sight of the cat frightened her, which resulted in the vision being fused together in her mind. The result: the next time the little girl saw a cat, the fear of the thunder was re-established. The fear was compounded each time she saw a cat. A few simple techniques in hypnosis enabled the client to change her behaviour, resulting in the end of the phobia. This illustrates how the mind works in creating new behaviours, as it is very literal. Fears and phobias can also be resolved with well-worded suggestion scripts in self-hypnosis without the intervention of a professional hypnotherapist.

From my extensive research, I have also found that not only is self-hypnosis proven to be a standalone therapeutic solution but it is also an excellent addition to all forms of therapy. Many studies have shown that using self-hypnosis between psychotherapy or counselling sessions strengthens the work. In fact, in the early 1990s when I was a consultant hypnotherapist at The Priory, a famous private hospital where the rich and famous sometimes seek treatment, I worked with psychiatrists and psychologists using hypnosis to overcome strong addictions and disorders, such as OCD (obsessive compulsive disorder), and they were able to note the huge benefits.

But self-hypnosis can also be used to facilitate positive life changes such as more confidence, accelerated learning, improved sports performance or ability, concentration, and even improving relationships. In Chapter 9 you'll find a selection of tried-and-tested scripts that you can use. You'll also learn how to form your own suggestions for any problem by following some simple guidelines in Chapter 6.

Case study

Mike Garside contacted me before setting off in the Whitbread Race, which involves competitors sailing single-handedly around the world. His main fear was that battling bad weather conditions and being on 'watch' for days on end could leave him exhausted, and he might sleep so soundly that he wouldn't wake up if the boat was in danger. He knew if that happened, his small boat could sink and he could die. He had already read my book *Free Yourself From Fear* and had practised self-hypnosis. However, he wanted to be able to go into a deeper hypnotic state. The problem was that I only had a single one-hour session with him before he flew off to start the race. He spent that hour repeatedly going into hypnosis until he achieved the depth he wanted. I created some specially worded suggestions for him and it worked wonders. He no longer had the fear and was even able to help another sailor over the radio during the race. He came in third and it was a privilege to cheer him back to shore in Charleston, USA.

Hypnosis and medicine

When I learned how to go into what I call the 'Nth phase', an almost hibernation state that requires no more than two breaths a minute, I was able to work with my friend's daughter who was in a coma. Her husband had been told to prepare himself for the worst, as her condition was serious and it was unlikely she would recover. Since she was in the emergency room wired up to life-support machines we were able to prove the effectiveness of this hypnosis intervention by the precise time shown on the machines when she started to recover.

Another client called late at night to tell me that he needed a serious operation the next day. However, the hospital had told him that the operation couldn't go ahead until his blood pressure was lower. The problem was that the surgeon was being flown in especially for the operation. James, my husband, who teaches medical hypnosis, went straight to the hospital and taught him how to use self-hypnosis to help him relax and reduce his blood pressure. The result was that the life-saving operation was able to go ahead, but only due to the use of self-hypnosis to affect his blood pressure.

Hyp-notes

As published in the media in 2002, a Stanford research study undertaken in 2000 supported the belief that hypnosis can transform perception and fully *proved* that hypnosis worked. By the use of PET scans to monitor neural activity, researchers demonstrated that the brain processes visual input differently under hypnosis – allowing subjects to 'see' colour when they are actually staring at a black image. By bolstering the idea that hypnosis transforms perception, the study supports the use of the technique to improve athletic and intellectual performance and even to 'think away' pain.[4]

David Spiegel MD, professor of psychiatry and behavioural sciences and senior author on the study, believes hypnosis to be a genuine mental state, in which our perception of reality changes and our mind 'like a telephoto lens zooms in on a subject', whereas sceptics thought it was just placebo or imagination.

Spiegel showed that hypnosis is a real neurological phenomenon, resulting in being able to help people modulate their perceptions in ways that can be therapeutically helpful. In *The Lancet* he and his colleagues reported that self-hypnosis could ease pain for patients receiving radiation treatment and that the patients who learned self-hypnosis not only reported feeling less pain, they used half the amount of pain medication, 'because they were able to change their perception of pain'.[7]

Of course hypnosis has been researched and proven effective for centuries but it helps to see some technical proof.

Whilst more complex medical issues require a skilled hypnotherapist to help resolve them, once learned, self-hypnosis can be used to reduce your blood pressure, reduce bleeding or pain in the dentist's chair, or even enable surgery without anaesthesia.

Case study

Soon after training with me, one of the therapists needed root canal dental work and was suffering terrible toothache. Everyone told him the procedure would be painful and he would be in agony for days afterwards. So he immediately set about using self-hypnosis for pain relief, and a visualization that the nerve connection would be like the wire inside an electrical fuse that had blown, i.e. that there was a visible gap between the two ends of the wire, meaning he wouldn't feel the pain, as it couldn't jump the gap. He underwent the surgery in a light trance, staring out of the window at a tree blowing in the wind, completely relaxed and with very little pain or discomfort. Everything healed quickly and the next day there was no pain at all.

Irish surgeon and hypnotherapist Dr Jack Gibson, with whom I trained, performed over 3,000 operations during his career using only hypnosis for painless surgery. He showed me a film of one of his patients who had had her leg amputated while under hypnosis. She had had her other leg amputated without hypnosis and suffered terrible phantom limb pain and excessive blood flow. None of this happened with the hypnosis, and she actually says in the film: 'If I had to have another leg off I would do it with hypnosis.' Dr Gibson said, 'You cannot pretend you are not in pain if I am sawing your leg off.'

Case study

There is a fascinating case of a surgeon who performed surgery on himself under self-hypnosis, and while standing. What is incredible is that if a patient is put in this position it could cause hypotension and shock. The surgeon had the procedure videotaped and explained everything thoroughly although it extended the operation to four hours, which is a very long time to be in trance. Even more impressive is that the surgeon took a drink of coffee halfway through his operation to show how well it was going.

Not only was there a reduction in the bleeding, swelling and scarring, but also the surgeon did not seem to be in pain during the operation. What's more, viewing himself a few feet above his body looking down onto his abdominal area, he performed the highly skilled surgery on his upper and lower abdomen and flank area while maintaining trance. He did this with simple self-hypnosis. Hypnoanesthesia for surgery is well documented in the *American Journal of Clinical Hypnosis*.[8]

A few years ago I began working with cancer sufferers and this eventually led to me co-producing a 90-minute feature documentary film, *The Face of Cancer*, which was screened at the Cannes Film Festival. The film enabled me to update my thinking on how very powerful the use of self-hypnosis is for physical problems as well as psychological problems. Since hypnosis relaxes both the mind and body automatically, just a few minutes a day using the inductions and exercises for trance in this book can help the healing process or reduce the pain of even terminally ill patients. And that is without even using suggestions, just pure relaxation.

Case study

When my close friend Inger, a criminal attorney, was diagnosed with stage four breast cancer, her specialist told her to put her affairs in order because it was that serious. In a desperate attempt to help Inger, I revisited all the research because I knew self-hypnosis had been successful in treating cancer at the turn of the century, so I started to look at how this could be used to save my friend's life. Normally, hypnotherapists work with cancer sufferers to relieve their stress, help them sleep, maintain a positive attitude, help them have the enthusiasm to eat healthily and help reduce the side effects of chemo and radiotherapy. My solution was to train Inger to use self-hypnosis to work with her subconscious to reduce the tumour until she could have the operation to remove it.

Inger wasn't able to have her operation for 60 days because of various delays. But she used self-hypnosis on herself for several hours each and every day without fail, and shrank the tumour to a smaller size by creating the image of a large egg in her mind to hold the cancer and stop it spreading.

By the time Inger had the operation, the tumour had reduced to half its size. To her surgeon's amazement not only had she reduced her diagnosis to stage two cancer – incredible in itself – but the 'egg' image had actually materialized and was holding the cancer. As she said in her testimonials 'Hypnosis saved my life.' Self-hypnosis had also enabled Inger to change her diet to be healthier and mainly organic. She continues to use self-hypnosis techniques and, thankfully, is now in remission.

So how does hypnosis feel?

The first major obstacle in determining how hypnosis feels is that there is no 'feeling' in hypnosis, just as there is no feeling when you go into a daydream. So how do you know when you are hypnotized? The fact is that you don't. You may have seen people in a hypnosis stage show perform extraordinary tasks but when brought out of trance refuse to believe they were in hypnosis at all. So the person who is working with hypnotizing themself needs to accept that it is unlikely they will have any feelings in hypnosis except that of relaxation.

The exception is when the subconscious may have taken a suggestion on board from something read earlier or spoken in hypnosis. For example, it could be indicating there may be a feeling or tingling sensation that is hypnosis. The person may not have any memory of hearing this information but it only presents itself when they are hypnotized and they experience a tingling.

It was common practice for a hypnotist to use this as a suggestibility test. Those who said they felt a slight tingling had accepted the suggestion and were therefore suggestible. Those who felt nothing had not accepted it, and were therefore not considered suggestible. However, they could still experience a similar quality of hypnosis if they persevered and had more practice.

So how do you know you've been in hypnosis? Well, everyone's experience is different. I could give you a list of physical signs that someone is in hypnosis but these can only be verified with a third party. Some people feel as though they've had a good relaxing sleep and awaken feeling refreshed and revitalized. However, these signs could be attributed to good-quality relaxation. A good indication is 'time distortion', where you think you've been in hypnosis for five minutes but in fact you've been in a trance state for almost an hour.

However, the real test is the effectiveness of the suggestions you use in self-hypnosis. If you notice that subtle (or unsubtle!) changes are occurring – for example you feel less stressed when faced with X situation or have lost weight or given up smoking – then you've been successfully hypnotized. This won't be the case with relaxation alone.

The good thing about hypnosis is that it is safe, without any negative side effects, and all human beings are able to obtain a hypnotic trance.

Depth of trance in self-hypnosis

As discussed earlier in the chapter, it is not always necessary to achieve a deep trance state for suggestions to be successful but it is considered to be more reliable, especially with pain relief. A deep trance brings deep relaxation so it can also be very healing. The reason for this is that muscle pain and tension, such as headaches and migraines, can be due to continual stress in your back, causing muscles to tighten automatically. Hypnosis can allow the body to relieve this tension fully for the period you are in a trance state. And with good hypnosis and direct suggestions it can have a lasting effect, giving the body a chance to heal itself.

I would like to emphasize that you should practise, practise, practise to get the deepest trance you can. Some people experience a good deep hypnosis straight away without any need to work at it but it is usually gained by going in and out of trance on a regular basis until you achieve a good deep hypnosis. Just remember that even while learning to go into deep hypnosis you will be reaping its positive benefits, as even the lightest trance can have a beneficial effect on your health by reducing your stress levels and helping you stay more present.

Once you have experienced a very deep trance, then there is no need for more practice as you can use this (automatically remembered) trance state to introduce your suggestions or just have a very healthy 'mind quiet'. It is rather like riding a bike; once you get your balance you're able to ride your bike and the skill is there forever, permanently implanted in your memory.

When the body is relaxed, your mental and emotional feelings will be more subdued. These are the first steps in 'letting go' of tension by creating muscle limpness. You may wonder what the term means and wonder 'letting go of what'? It really means letting go of tension. A lot of us don't realize how tense we are and many have become habitually tense without realizing it. In fact in some cases this overactive state has become a normal condition. The body gives out signs of tension by frowning, blinking and fidgeting, which indicate your need to de-stress. Relaxation is nothing more than an absence of tension and your purpose is to reduce the tension to a minimum. To give you an example, if you concentrate on relaxing your face muscles you will realize how rarely you relax these muscles.

As you start to learn the skills of self-hypnosis, you will find it a wonderful experience, but do be aware that only a small percentage of people go deep the first time they use it. So it's important to read the relevant chapters before you begin practising putting yourself into trance, as this will build your beliefs and knowledge about self-hypnosis. Each of the chapters gives a brief history, proven facts and detailed case-history evidence and these will be your building blocks to maximizing your hypnotic potential. You don't want to be the person who says, 'It didn't work for me', thinking you weren't hypnotizable when a little time could make all the difference. So bear with me, and I will take you on a learning journey that will help you get the very best out of your deep trance hypnosis.

Hyp-notes

Stage hypnotists use induction techniques that quickly induce hypnosis. However, it's worth noting that these techniques are limited and only work on a small selection of volunteers – usually about a third of any audience who are susceptible and can be hypnotized straight away. Before the hypnotist does the instant induction they will do a suggestibility test. A popular test is to ask the audience to clasp their hands together while suggesting, very quickly and repeatedly, they cannot pull their hands apart. The ones who can't are considered susceptible and will be the ones that are invited to be a part of the act.

A quick induction technique is all-important to the stage hypnotist because time is of the essence, or the audience would very quickly get bored. On the other hand, the hypnotherapist, someone that uses specific techniques to bring about positive change while their client is in hypnosis, generally has the luxury of time, so will usually choose a more relaxing way to induce their clients into hypnosis. These longer inductions have to work with both the susceptible and the not-so-susceptible subjects.

Improving concentration

I have been training hypnotherapists for over 25 years but in the last few years I have witnessed a vast change in concentration and focus. With modern technology we are forever multitasking using smartphones and other devices on the go. Our minds never get the chance to rest, apart from when we're asleep. Even then people find it difficult to get a good night's sleep as we are overloaded with thoughts running round our heads. It is now more important than ever to retrain your mind to focus, so you can experience deep relaxation. Concentration and focus are key elements in learning how to use self-hypnosis effectively and as you practise you'll discover they will automatically improve. Everyone can benefit from a quieter mind and it can have a dramatic effect on your health and wellbeing.

To help you, I have included some simple mind exercises in Chapter 4, which are designed to help you learn to direct your concentration on the single task of deep relaxation. Using these exercises in hypnosis will greatly speed up your learning process. There is no 'right' or 'wrong' way to do them, so if you need more practice to reach a depth of trance with self-hypnosis that is fine. Some people need more time to learn a language or drive a car than others but most people get there in the end.

Using the mind exercises will help you speed up the process of hypnosis, so that you can focus on creating your personal suggestions to make your changes. You'll also learn how to use the simple language of the subconscious to create that perfect suggestion for what you wish to achieve. Whatever you want to use self-hypnosis for, these instructions are your first steps to manifesting your life change.

The next chapter gives you a more detailed understanding about self-hypnosis before you start practising it. I have known clients who don't follow my instructions for self-hypnosis and then wonder why something didn't work. So please take the time to read everything carefully and you won't be disappointed with the results you can achieve, as these methods are tried and tested. You'll find useful checklists at the end of each of the following chapters if you need a quick reminder of what you have learned.

RECAP ✍

❖ Hypnosis is an altered state of consciousness, in which you are deeply relaxed and so able to access and make suggestions to your subconscious.

❖ Deep trances take practice, belief and understanding, so increasing your knowledge about how self-hypnosis works will improve your chances of success, and this book is designed to help you do this.

❖ Hypnosis can help treat a range of medical issues but is particularly noted in helping relaxation, 'letting go' and improving concentration.

❖ The limitless power of self-hypnosis can change your life and even bring about positive changes in your personality.

❖ Belief is important in maximizing your skill in self-hypnosis. Just like Couè's patients who believed that medicine worked because it was dispensed by someone they respected. Medical placebos work because people believe they will.

Chapter 3
Visualization and creating big dreams

'"Impossible" only means "I-M-Possible", and "No" only means "Next Option".'

YOSSI GHINSBERG

What do you want? Do you know? Once you recognize it, you can give your subconscious a set of instructions to follow. After all, you don't want to be running down the wrong road and not realize it until you get there, so it's important to know what you're setting out to achieve. Expand your awareness by taking away all the limitations then see what you would really like for yourself. Then look at your life as it is now and see what you can do to make it work for you. This is the first step in making goals: once you know what you would really like to do you can make a plan and a timescale.

Imagination in trance is the language to your inner mind. Instruct it to do what 'you' want.

Next you need to plant the seeds of your goals in your subconscious so that it will bring in opportunities to help you achieve those goals. You might choose to do this by scanning magazines or the Internet for pictures that represent your goals; for example, a picture of your favourite car, a person that is an ideal weight or has a healthy glow, or the place you'd like to live. Now position those images where you can see them all the time; for example, on the fridge or on your desktop. Many of the most successful people in the world have used this simple method and it is the core of Napoleon Hill's book *Think and Grow Rich*, which I also recommend you read as part of your goal-setting strategy.

Use the pictures to help remind you of the promotion you want, the business you intend to build, how you would like to look, how you would like to be, etc. Each time you look at the image it will serve as a reminder of your goals and pretty soon that image will be imprinted in your mind.

Now, your inner mind will have a direction and start to give you ideas of how you can achieve your goals. Ideas will just pop into your mind and when you follow them it will lead you to other opportunities that you wouldn't normally have thought possible.

For example, if you choose to buy a classic car it is common sense that you would search out places you can buy classic cars, i.e. going to outlets that sell or show classic cars. You won't be interested in other garages and showrooms that have cars that you don't want, as that is not what you have chosen to have. You are just focused on looking in the right places and you do this without too much thought. Actually you have made your decision and your inner mind is now directed to give you thoughts that lead you to find classic cars.

Planning your future works

Wishing is what we do, so we can create goals and focus our mind on making them come true. There is even proof of it. Dr Edwin Locke did some pioneering research on goal setting and motivation in the late 1960s. In his 1968 article 'Toward a Theory of Task Motivation and Incentives', he stated that employees were motivated by clear goals and appropriate feedback. Locke went on to say that working towards a goal provided a major source of motivation to actually reaching the goal – which, in turn, improved performance.

More than 50 years later, his ideas are no longer revolutionary but very workable and used by the majority of successful people. Locke's research also showed that there was a relationship between how difficult and specific a goal was and how people performed. He was surprised to find that difficult goals led to better performance than vague or easy goals.

A few years later researcher Dr Gary Latham studied the effect of goal setting in the workplace. His results supported Locke's findings and the link between goal setting and performance was formed. In 1990, Locke and Latham published their seminal work, *A Theory of Goal Setting and Task Performance*. In this book, they stress the importance of setting specific and difficult goals. However, there is a conflict in what these studies showed and what is found to be possible. They say it is important to strike an appropriate balance between a challenging goal and a realistic goal. They suggest that setting a goal that you'll fail to achieve is possibly more demotivating than setting a goal that's too easy. But now people are finding that they can achieve what was once thought of as impossible. For example, at one time, the four-minute mile was thought to be an impossible feat, but now many athletes have run a mile in less than three minutes.

You might have heard of the SMART technique for setting goals, which is still popular in business for measuring employee success. Smart goals are supposed to be 'specific, measurable, achievable, relevant and time-related'. But in setting your goals please don't be bound by what is 'achievable', as when you bring the power of the mind into play anything is possible. We have limitless potential and once you start to visualize your dreams and work with your unconscious you may find, as I did, that anything is indeed possible.

Hyp-notes

In 1908, Andrew Carnegie interviewed Napoleon Hill. Hill had big dreams of being a lawyer, and to pay his way through law school he planned to interview successful men and women and write about how they became successful, for the popular magazines of the day. Carnegie encouraged him but said that it would take 20 years of effort, and he might not get recognition for his work for many years after it was published. Hill took the challenge and with a letter of introduction from Carnegie began a long journey that resulted in one of the best-selling books in history, which has sold more than 70 million copies: *Think and Grow Rich*.

Hill not only interviewed 50 of the most important, successful men of the time, including Theodore Roosevelt, Thomas Edison, John D. Rockefeller, Henry Ford, Alexander Graham Bell, and King Gillette (founder of the Gillette Safety Razor Company), which is well known, but he also interviewed over 500 people who had failed to achieve their goals.

Carnegie said, 'If you carry it through successfully, you will make a discovery which may be a great surprise to you.' This makes a lot of sense since so many incredibly wealthy and successful people have 'rags to riches' stories, including Carnegie himself. He said that he believed that we are never so close to success as when we think failure has overtaken us and that failure is just a signal to 're-arm'.

For me, reading Hill's book in the early 1990s was revolutionary; I wrote down my plan on the 'goal sheet' as he suggested, did my visualizations in trance, repeated the affirmations and absorbed the chapter on self-hypnosis. I was extremely busy but very focused and success followed hard on its heels. In my first year as a hypnotherapist I made £100,000, which was a huge amount of money in 1990. If you read Hill's book, which I highly recommend, you will not only discover the power of self-hypnosis but also the keys to dreaming big and achieving your dreams.

When you identify goals that are most important to you, you can begin to figure out ways to make them come true. Your mind will give you thoughts and ideas on how you can change your attitudes, abilities, skills and financial earnings to reach them. You'll begin noticing new ways of doing things that you had never thought of before.

Remember the key is thinking. Put some time aside each day, perhaps just before you sleep or as soon as you wake up, to think and dream. Don't let your old ways stop you from visualizing your goals. Push out the negative thoughts that are old doubts and fears, so you can listen to reasonable thoughts. For example, expect to win or get the position you want. Expect to get a parking place convenient to you by picturing yourself parking happily and on time, etc. Put those expectations into visualizations as though it has happened and this will help jump-start your subconscious into action.

Just like learning to ride a bike, your mind will start to respond. If you don't always get what you wish for just pass it off as fate, which has a better road for you to follow. This will help prevent those old doubts creeping in. Just because Plan A doesn't work out immediately, don't let this stop you from putting Plan B into action.

Hyp-notes

Arnold Schwarzenegger is an excellent example of a person's perseverance, determination and having no limitations on his goals. At 21 he had made his way from a small town in Austria to Los Angeles where he won the title of Mr Universe. Arnold was a follower of Napoleon Hill and has used self-hypnosis to help him achieve his goals throughout his life.

In Arnold's early days, before he became a movie star and ultimately Governor of California, he said, 'Without mastery over your mind you will never have mastery over your body. I am convinced that you become what you think about most. Dwell on the negative thoughts and you fail. Dwell on the positive thoughts and you succeed. Had I believed there were actual physical limits to the potential size of my arms, they would never have gotten as big and muscular.'

To prove his point he added, 'Some people make remarks like "I would like a 20-inch arm someday" and then in the next breath, "But I could never do that." They have already defeated themselves by mentally setting limits.'[9]

He used a type of self-hypnosis as an everyday concept, which you can easily do now with the new technology that is available to us.

Goal-setting rules

Your focus and determination will put the vital positive energy into your *mind programs*. Once you begin the process you will start to have thoughts about how to achieve your goals and your inner mind will give you the help to focus your efforts and clearly define what you are going to do.

- ❖ Focus on what you want.

- ❖ Visualize yourself having it.

- ❖ Expect it to happen.

- ❖ Know precisely what you want to achieve.

- ❖ Know where you have to concentrate your efforts.

- ❖ Notice any old distractions that can take your mind off your goals. Just be disciplined and bring your mind back to your planning.

- ❖ Write all your goals down, as this will provide you with an additional focus and a reference for your achievements in the future. You can also use your list of goals for creating well-formed suggestions, which you will learn about in chapter 6.

❖ Remember, a goal properly set is halfway reached; as Émile Coué said, 'We actually make or mar our own health and destinies according to the ideas at work in our subconscious.'

How visual are you?

Creating images in your mind helps to focus your inner mind. It really is a key element in using self-hypnosis effectively. However, some people are more 'visual' than others; suggestions tend to include 'imagining' things and often people say they can't 'see' anything when asked to visualize.

If you thought of a party as a happy event, you'd get a picture or *thought* in your mind of you being happy and enjoying yourself. The opposite is also true. If you thought of something as being not so pleasant, you'd picture yourself being miserable.

So, here's a simple test to see how visual you are. Close your eyes and think of a chair. Imagine what colour it is and what it's made of. Did you see a picture or did you just know what it looked like? You'll instinctively know without analysing anything. So, when you are doing self-hypnosis, just relax and visualize things as you did with the chair. There's no right way or wrong way to do it, because everyone is different. Some people see things in their imagination while others just know what it looks like.

Quality of life: plan for a better future

This is a simple but very effective method of making some incredible changes you didn't think possible with only a couple of minutes twice a day. This short time allows you to reprogram your mind to attain your goals. If you persevere for three weeks it will become a habit and you won't be surprised to notice many incredible improvements in your life.

When you have succeeded in using self-hypnosis effectively, a quick daily input of three impact words, that literally takes seconds, will start to energize your desired changes – without the need for lengthy suggestions.

Find three powerful words that epitomize the changes you want, dynamic words, e.g. successful, dynamic, charismatic, fully confident, etc. Choose three words that you feel realize your wishes.

When you have the words, quickly put yourself into self-hypnosis and access your subconscious by instructing it to come forward in the form of a picture or a thought. You can use the same picture or thought each time if you feel comfortable, or wait for one to come at random.

Now say the three words privately in your mind, and as you say them picture yourself on a large TV screen behaving in this way. Make sure you add detail to ensure you really illustrate to your subconscious mind what those three words really mean to you.

Then just open your eyes.

Do this every day for at least three weeks and you will start to see changes in your attitudes. It is a simple blueprint for improvement. The rehearsal in your mind is important to show your subconscious just what you want. When you practise self-hypnosis you will soon be able to just close your eyes and go immediately into hypnosis, so this method is very quick and powerful.

RECAP ✍

❖ Wishes and planning for your future using powerful images fuel the imagination in your subconscious mind.

❖ Napoleon Hill recognized the power of using self-hypnosis to help create your future.

❖ Remember to follow the goal setting rules to create a blueprint before creating your suggestions.

❖ You can plan for a better future using a few powerful words repeated daily.

❖ Imagination is the language of the subconscious.

PART II
SELF-HYPNOSIS TECHNIQUES AND SCRIPTS

'You cannot be happy and sad at the same time – so you have a choice – and self-hypnosis gives you that incredible control over your life.'

Chapter 4
How to hypnotize yourself

'Vision without execution is delusion.'
THOMAS EDISON

In this chapter, you'll learn to use my step-by-step, easy-to-follow Progressive Relaxation induction to hypnotize yourself. I have used this method for self-hypnosis for over 25 years, so it has had rigorous testing and is the ideal way to start your training into deep trance hypnosis. Not all things that are new are better.

Hypnosis is anything but black and white and certainly not always logical. Generally a 'deep' trance can equal good-quality hypnosis therapy, but not always. Some people only ever experience a light trance but can still experience the extraordinary benefits of self-hypnosis.

Remember, the behaviours and issues you want to change may have been around for most of your life, so repeated listening to your suggestions is more often required to bring about the changes you desire. It is likely you'll notice subtle changes in behaviour or attitudes, which then bring about bigger changes in your life. Realizing that self-hypnosis has brought about these changes will encourage you to listen to the suggestion again.

Checklist for self-hypnosis

It is important to prepare yourself for your self-hypnosis, so make sure you have read the earlier chapters to give you the information you will need. Taking the following steps should help you prepare your mind and body for self-hypnosis. I have purposely covered a variety of common problems that may occur, which could disturb your hypnosis.

❖ Find a quiet place to sit or lie down and a comfortable chair, lounger, bed or even the floor.

❖ Check that you do not need the bathroom.

❖ Dim the lights or close the curtains.

❖ Check mobiles, tablets or phones are switched off and you are unlikely to be disturbed. Don't forget to turn your computer sound off so you are not disturbed by the sound of Skype calls or email alerts.

❖ The room temperature should be comfortable with no draughts but you might want to cover yourself with a blanket, especially if you generally feel chilly when sleepy.

❖ Check your neck is in a comfortable position. Use a pillow if necessary, and a small flat cushion may be useful in the small of your back. If you are lying down, you may want to put a cushion behind your knees and place your hands at your sides without touching your body.

❖ Close your eyes, as this will make it easier to focus on the relaxation techniques (although it's not always necessary as some inductions may start by having the eyes open).

✦ Take a few deep breaths before you start and prepare your mind to be fully involved in the self-hypnosis process.

✦ Remember hypnosis is not a passive act but will require your full involvement.

✦ Approach hypnosis with an uncritical acceptance, which will allow the suggestions you have chosen to be accepted. In other words don't analyse what you hear during the induction. If you have trained in NLP or other types of mind-analysing therapies, try to leave your knowledge outside the door so that your conscious mind remains aware but quiet during the induction. Your inner mind will naturally filter out what is not necessary.

✦ If your mind starts to wander during the induction (for example, thinking about your shopping list or what you have to do after the hypnosis or even the next day) just bring your thoughts back to concentrating on your chosen induction. It is your responsibility to discipline your mind. One way of doing this is just to focus your awareness on your breathing whilst continuing to listen to the induction. If you attend to any wandering thoughts immediately, you'll find your mind soon learns a new habit and your focus and concentration become much easier and more natural to attain.

✦ Finally, self-hypnosis is meant to be used when you are relaxed and can focus your attention on it so do not listen to any self-hypnosis recordings when driving or operating machinery.

Easy ways to practise self-hypnosis

Practice is particularly important, as you will have your own personal depth of trance when you first hypnotize yourself. If you have experienced hypnosis before then it is also a good opportunity to add more depth to your trance. If you follow these few simple guidelines you will soon be able to achieve a good state of hypnosis, but you must follow the instructions. Like all habits and mind teachings, the more you practise, the deeper and more satisfying your hypnosis will become. The benefits will become obvious as you find yourself going into self-hypnosis quickly and easily.

1. Letting go and mind discipline

In the next chapter, you'll find a range of exercises to help you learn the art of 'letting go', which simply means going along with the process without your conscious mind interrupting. With practice you'll be able to experience an amazing feeling I call 'mind quiet', in which your mind clears and becomes free of nagging thoughts and conscious ideas. For the moment, however, keep your mind on the words and what you should be doing. If your mind wanders, immediately bring it back to concentrating on the induction or the suggestions and soon your inner mind will begin to get into the habit of relaxing and 'letting go'.

You don't have to go into a deep trance for suggestions to be accepted by your subconscious, but generally it is thought that the suggestions will be more effective. I recommend you persevere so you can achieve the best possible results. Repetition is also essential in self-hypnosis and was the key ingredient in Coué's autosuggestions (*see pages 8–9*). Repeat your self-hypnosis once a day, every day, or twice a day if you can. The more you practise, the better chance you have of succeeding.

> *Remember, if your mind wanders when*
> *going into trance, immediately bring*
> *it back to listening to the words.*

2. Breathing

Breathing deeply and rhythmically is most relaxing, and concentrating on your breathing can, in itself, start to induce a light trance. Your breath should feel comfortable and easy for you. Try taking a few deep breaths or breathing deeply before starting your induction and you'll notice your body relaxing automatically. Your breathing normally slows down and may become shallower as you go into trance.

3. Record your induction

There are various ways of hypnotizing yourself, but the most popular way is by recording yourself and then playing it back when you are sitting or lying comfortably and ready to go into hypnosis. Recording is much easier now as most smartphones generally have a recording app; otherwise a digital recorder can be purchased separately. You then simply record yourself (or ask someone to do it for you) reading the Progressive Relaxation induction.

When recording your voice, you need to be slow and monotonous, speaking very slowly and distinctly. It is useful to highlight important words or phrases with your voice tone. If you decide to ask someone else to record the hypnosis scripts (e.g. a friend with a good recording voice), you should tell them to speak with a monotonous, gentle voice.

As you get more used to practising self-hypnosis you can choose from the many induction scripts in this book and those on www.selfhypnosisthebook.com, which I have developed especially to accompany this book. It includes the audio recordings for the Progressive Relaxation induction (*see page 51*) and the Orange Liquid suggestion (*see page 57*) for you to use if you are finding it difficult to record the inductions yourself. You can choose from inductions that take you by the sea, on a boat, or on a magical journey – the list is endless and caters for everyone. Some people may love being by the sea whereas others may have a fear of drowning and would not find the water very relaxing. I personally find that being in a garden seems to satisfy most people and use it as the first induction into hypnosis.

As I mentioned above, the Progressive Relaxation induction is available on the website; however, it really is worth recording it yourself, as it only takes about six–eight minutes to record and your own voice may carry some added energy. To help you read the scripts in this book, I have added spacing in the form of three spaced dots between certain words and phrases so you know when to leave pauses and where words should be highlighted for more effect. There will be more pauses in hypnosis scripts on purpose as they are more a collection of subtle instructions.

Recording your induction checklist

❖ Speak clearly in a monotonous tone, in a voice that is soothing and not too loud, but loud enough for you to hear.

❖ Allow a short time at the beginning of the recording so you have time to get comfortable on your bed or in a chair.

❖ Notice that the grammar in inductions or suggestions does not always have to be precise, as it is a special subconscious language. Words creating confusion may occur but it is part of the 'controlled confusion' that helps the hypnotic trance. To help you devise your own suggestion just imagine you are reciting it to a five-year-old child and ask yourself if they would be able to understand it. If the answer is 'yes' you are on the right path.

4. Learn your induction

Some people might find learning a script takes a lot of energy while others may prefer this to recording; it makes no difference and is your choice as both recording and learning can lead to the same outcome. If you do decide to learn the Progressive Relaxation induction word-for-word, close your eyes, take a few slow deep breaths and begin. You can talk to yourself aloud or silently using the first or second person. For example, changing the word 'you' to 'I' will not make a difference, it is only a matter of choice. Do your self-talk slowly and with feeling. When you have finished, you can allow yourself some quiet time or use this time to go to sleep. Otherwise recite the 'count out' of hypnosis (see below) or just gently open your eyes.

The words need to be learned precisely or they may not be as effective. The most successful way to make sure the words are correct is when you have learned them and feel comfortable with them, take the time to write the whole script down – then check you have them absolutely correct. Note: don't hypnotize yourself until you have them all correct, if you want maximum impact.

Time to begin

Below you'll find a variety of self-hypnosis techniques to choose from but I suggest you start with the Progressive Relaxation induction first and then progress to other methods once you feel comfortable with the process of self-hypnosis. The reason for this is that the Progressive Relaxation induction not only induces hypnosis, but also allows you to work on systematically relaxing your body. This can be especially useful if, at any time, you have problems getting to sleep, as you can either play the recording or recite it to yourself before you go to sleep. It will occupy your mind so you are not continually going over problems in your head that might otherwise keep you awake. If you skip this important training you may miss out on a very basic and classic method, which has been proven to be highly effective.

How often you want to start practising self-hypnosis is entirely personal but I strongly recommend you try it daily **for at least three weeks** to develop a new habit. Regular practice will quickly increase the quality of the results you get.

Once you have recorded or learned the Progressive Relaxation induction you can then add your chosen suggestion scripts. I have included some general scripts later on in this chapter, but you'll also find a selection of suggestions for common problems and life improvement in Chapter 9. Additionally, you can create your own suggestions using the guidelines in Chapter 6.

Remember, the Progressive Relaxation induction can be used whenever you want some deep relaxation or mind quiet. Alternatively, you can add your chosen suggestion to the end. The Orange Liquid suggestion (*see page 57*) is more for a clean-out, or deep-stress release.

The Progressive Relaxation induction script

In this deep, and special sleep . . . your subconscious mind . . . for your safekeeping . . . monitors everything that is happening around you . . . Therefore these suggestions, because they are for your benefit, go directly to your subconscious mind . . . where they are accepted . . . These thoughts become established . . . firmly fixed . . . deeply . . . in your inner mind . . . Embedded, so these suggestions remain with you . . . long after you open your eyes . . . Helping you to change those things you want to change, for your own sake . . . And these new thoughts . . . help you begin to change the things you want to change . . . And these changes allow you to enjoy your life . . . more . . . and . . . more . . .

I want you to imagine that you're checking your body to ensure you become totally relaxed . . . as your muscles relax . . . just let your mind relax also . . . begin with your feet . . . feel your toes . . . stretch them . . .

*feel the texture of what your feet are resting on . . .
begin to tighten your calves . . . now relax them . . .
let that relaxation spread past your ankles . . . up
your calves to the back of your knees . . . feel those
muscles easing . . . resting comfortably . . . now your
thighs . . . pull them tight . . . be aware of those long
muscles tensing . . . now relax those muscles . . . feel
them lengthening and resting comfortably . . . feel
your legs as they sink even deeper into the cushions*
[personalize, depending upon where you will be using
the induction] *as you relax even more . . . and notice
how rhythmic your breathing is becoming . . . now your
stomach muscles . . . pull them together gently . . .
now let them expand and relax comfortably.*

*Your shoulders and back muscles . . . flex your
shoulders . . . feel those muscles pull across your
back . . . now let your shoulders slouch as you relax the
muscles . . . and notice how your spine sinks deeper
into your chair, as you relax even more deeply . . .
notice how easy and regular your breathing has
become . . . Now your fingertips . . . and fingers . . .
clench them . . . feel that tension . . . now relax them . . .
and allow the relaxation to spread up your arms to
your neck . . . Make sure your neck is comfortable,
with your head in an easy position . . . tighten up your
neck muscles . . . now let those columns of muscles
loosen . . . as the muscles relax allow your neck to sink
into the cushions into a comfortable position.*

*Your face muscles are flat and stretch comfortably
across your face . . . squeeze up your face . . . and feel
the tension . . . now relax those muscles and feel them*

*lengthening . . . and softening . . . relaxing . . . more than
ever before.*

*You can now feel the air temperature against your
skin . . . It feels smooth and comfortable . . . now you
can allow the relaxation to spread to your scalp . . .
knowing that you are relaxed throughout your body . . .
from the top of your head . . . to the tips of your toes.*

*Your body is now loose . . . and limp . . . and heavy . . .
and relaxed . . . notice how your body is sinking
deeper into relaxation . . . as your breathing becomes
more regular and easy . . . in a moment I will count
slowly from one . . . to ten . . . and with each number
you drift . . . deeper . . . and deeper . . . into peaceful
relaxation . . .* [counting slowly and deliberately]
*one . . . two . . . three . . . four . . . five . . . six . . . seven . . .
eight . . . nine . . . ten.*

*You are now feeling so deeply relaxed . . . you find it
easy to focus your attention . . . and imagine things
very clearly . . . and I want you to imagine that you
are standing on a balcony . . . which has steps leading
down to a beautiful garden . . . as you look into the
garden . . . you see that it is surrounded with lovely
trees . . . ensuring the garden is private . . . secluded
and peaceful . . . There are flower beds . . . set in the
lovely lawn . . . and further along is a waterfall . . .
flowing into a stream . . . Listen to the sound of the
water . . . as you look around . . . you see the trees . . .
and you hear a faint sound of a bird in the distance . . .
adding to the feeling of deep . . . relaxation . . . through
your entire being . . . If you look more closely you*

will see that there are five steps leading down to the garden . . . and then a small path . . . that leads to the waterfall . . . In a moment we will walk down the steps . . . and with each step you go deeper . . . and deeper into relaxation . . .

So let's begin.

As you put your foot on the first step you feel yourself going deeper into relaxation . . . down on to the second step . . . and as you feel your foot firmly placed on the step . . . you feel a wonderful relief . . . as you drift even deeper into relaxation . . . down on to the third step . . . feeling wonderfully free and . . . so . . . so . . . relaxed . . . as your foot reaches for the fourth step . . . another wave of relaxation drifts through your whole body . . . down on to the fifth step now . . . and feeling even more deeply relaxed than ever before.

Now as you find yourself standing on the lawn . . . you see a little way ahead . . . a waterfall . . . listen to the water as it gently splashes . . . you can notice the birds singing in the distance . . . and the sound of the trees gently swaying . . . and a little to the side is a comfortable garden bench . . . Notice the colour of the bench . . . what it is made of?

In a moment I would like you to walk over to the bench . . . and sit down on the bench . . . When you sit down you will be surprised at how comfortable it is . . . and then you will be even more relaxed than you are now . . . so let's begin to walk over . . . [leave a short pause] . . . now sit down on the bench . . . and as you sit down on the bench . . . take a deep breath . . . and as you breathe out . . . you feel a wave of relaxation go through your body . . . relaxing every muscle and nerve . . . As you breathe in . . . you breathe in positive thoughts . . . and as you breathe out . . . you breathe out negative thoughts . . . leaving room for more positive thoughts.

You may want to just drift into sleep . . . and if you just want to go to sleep you can just ignore the next few words . . . and rather than count you out of hypnosis they will just seem to lull you into a deep and comfortable sleep . . . until it is your time to awaken. However, if it is time for you to awaken from hypnosis . . . You will use these words . . . to awaken you . . . from this deep and comfortable hypnosis . . . in a moment I will count from ten to one . . . and at the count of one . . . you will be fully aware and refreshed and your eyes will open . . . [counting slowly and deliberately] *Ten . . . nine . . . eight . . . coming up now . . . seven . . . six . . . five . . . more and more aware . . . four . . . three . . . two . . . one . . . LET YOUR EYES OPEN.*

Note: If you want to use the Progressive Relaxation induction before you go to sleep you can leave the audio playing with a period of silence at the end and let the system switch itself off. If you find you are sleeping almost immediately this is fine, as the script will still continue being processed.

Counting out of hypnosis

Some people will just naturally open their eyes when they are ready to come out of hypnosis. However, the following script is used to bring you out of relaxation slowly and soothingly. You can add it to the end of your chosen suggestion.

In a moment I will count from ten to one . . . and at the count of one . . . you will be fully aware and refreshed and your eyes will open and you will feel good about yourself . . . Ten . . . nine . . . eight . . . coming up now . . . seven . . . six . . . five . . . more and more aware . . . four . . . three . . . two . . . one . . . EYES OPEN.

Your personal de-stressor

In addition to the Progressive Relaxation induction, a deep de-stressor called Orange Liquid can also be used as an alternative induction or just as a suggestion. You should only use it once you've gained experience using the Progressive Relaxation induction, but it is an excellent way to clear away old doubts and fears. It is a sort of 'spring cleaning' for the mind, getting rid of the old negative mental programs, even from as long ago as childhood, which may be holding you back or affecting your stress levels. It is particularly useful during times of high stress or worry. You can also use it to deal with trauma-related or deep-seated problems.

Many hypnotherapists use the Orange Liquid suggestion when they are stressed or have major unexpected problems crop up. In fact, Orange Liquid was so effective that Deborah Marshall-Warren, whom I trained in the early 1990s, asked me if she could write a book based on my suggestion, which I had adapted from an old script in the

1980s. *Mind Detox* was so successful that Deborah was featured in a number of major newspapers and magazines and it launched her business.

Orange Liquid

You can start with just sitting or lying comfortably, closing your eyes and focusing on your breathing. Allow yourself to breathe rhythmically and comfortably deeply then listen to your recording.

You're resting comfortably now . . . you're calm and relaxed. In this state of calm and peace, you radiate more self-confidence . . . more love . . . more enjoyment of life because now you can free yourself of all the things that are holding you back . . . all the doubt . . . all the discomfort . . . all the fears. In your imagination, you can do or be whatever you wish to do or be. Through your imagination, you can free yourself of all the restrictions . . . all the limitations . . . all the negative thoughts that have accumulated over the years.

To do this, imagine now that your body is a large glass container that I'm going to fill with a soothing, warm, orange liquid . . . beginning at your toes and ending with your scalp . . . using your imagination, concentrate your awareness on your toes . . . now just imagine a warm, orange liquid moving in through your toes . . . feel the warm, orange liquid moving slowly through your toes and emptying into your feet . . . now feel your feet filling with a warm, orange liquid . . . filling your feet completely now . . . and moving up . . . up into your calves . . . now feel your calves filling with a warm, orange liquid . . . a soothing, tingling warmth filling your calves completely now . . . and moving up . . . up into your knees . . . now feel your knees filling with a warm, orange liquid . . . feel it moving in and out of your knees . . . moving through your knees and moving up . . . up into your thighs . . . now feel your thighs filling with a warm, orange liquid . . . a soothing, tingling warmth filling your thighs completely now . . . now feel that soothing, tingling warmth moving freely throughout your legs . . . becoming warmer and warmer as we continue.

Concentrate your awareness on your hands . . . now just imagine that same warm, orange liquid moving in through your fingertips . . . feel the warm, orange liquid moving slowly through your fingers and emptying into your hands . . . now feel your hands filling with a warm, orange liquid . . . filling your hands completely now . . . and moving up . . . up into your forearms . . . now feel your forearms filling with a warm, orange liquid . . . a soothing, tingling warmth filling your forearms completely now and moving up . . . up into your elbows . . . now feel your elbows filling with a warm, orange liquid . . . feel it moving in and out of your elbows . . . moving through your elbows and moving up . . . up into your arms . . . now feel your upper arms filling with a warm, orange liquid . . . a soothing, tingling warmth filling your upper arms completely now . . . now feel that soothing, tingling warmth moving freely throughout your arms and legs . . . becoming warmer and warmer as we continue.

Concentrate your awareness on your pelvic area . . . now feel a warm, orange liquid flowing in . . . feel your pelvic area filling with a warm, orange liquid . . . a soothing, tingling warmth filling your entire pelvic area . . . and moving up . . . up into your stomach . . . now feel your stomach filling with a warm, orange liquid . . . feel every muscle . . . every fibre . . . every nerve in your stomach, warm and relaxed now . . . warm and relaxed . . . feel your entire stomach area filled with a warm, orange liquid . . . and moving up, up into your chest . . . now feel your chest filling with a warm, orange liquid . . . a soothing, tingling warmth filling your entire chest cavity . . . and moving up . . . up into your shoulders . . . now feel your shoulders filling with a warm, orange liquid . . . filling your shoulders completely now and moving up . . . up into your neck . . . feel your neck filling with a warm, orange liquid . . . and moving up . . . up the back of your head . . . up into your jaws . . . and your jaws become relaxed . . . now feel the warm orange liquid moving up . . . up into your cheeks . . . and your cheeks begin to sag just a little . . . now feel the warm, orange liquid moving up into your eyes . . . and your eyes relax even more . . . now feel the warm, orange liquid moving up . . . up into your forehead . . . and your forehead becomes relaxed . . . now feel the warm, orange liquid moving all the way up to your scalp . . . filling your entire head area with a warm, orange liquid . . . a soothing, tingling warmth . . . just imagine your entire body and mind are filled with a warm, orange liquid . . . become aware of a soothing, tingling warmth moving freely throughout your body and mind.

Experience a few moments of silence, from my voice . . . Use your imagination . . . and just imagine you can feel the warm, orange liquid freeing your body and mind of all the restrictions . . . mental and physical . . . all the negative thoughts . . . all doubts . . . the fears . . . the discomfort . . . feel all of your limitations being absorbed and dissolved into the warm, orange liquid . . . until you next hear my voice . . .

[Pause for 60 seconds.]

Become aware of my voice now . . . become aware of my voice . . . and listen.

You're resting comfortably now . . . you are calm and relaxed . . . Your body and mind are filled with a warm, orange liquid . . . a soothing, tingling warmth . . . Use your imagination now and feel the warm, orange liquid dissolving and absorbing all the negativity in your body and mind . . . negativity comes in many forms . . . stress, tensions, anxiety . . . doubt, depression, discomfort . . . insecurity . . . fears of all kinds . . . Using your imagination, you can actually feel the warm, orange liquid working now . . . like a million little bubbles inside you scrubbing away . . . cleansing your body and mind from the inside out . . . cleaning it up . . . clearing away all the restrictions . . . all the limitations . . . all the negativity. Feel your body and mind being freed of all the negative feelings . . . all the negative thoughts . . . all the negative actions from the past . . . and the present . . . Physical or emotional problems will appear as darkened areas throughout the body and mind. . . Make a mental note of the darkened

*areas you are now aware of . . . now direct the warm,
liquid to those areas . . . feel it releasing the emotional
stress . . . all the suppressed feelings . . . all the pent-
up emotions . . . now feel it dissolving and absorbing
the physical discomforts . . . now concentrate your
awareness on those areas most easily influenced by
stress and tension . . . Your head area . . . your neck and
shoulders . . . your back . . . your stomach to name a
few . . . now feel a soothing, tingling warmth developing
in these areas . . . feel the stress and tension being
released through the gentle action of the warm, orange
liquid . . . Using your mind in a more creative way,
you've already released much of the stress and tension
responsible for many of your discomforts . . . As a result
of this with each new day, you're better able to cope
with everyday pressures at home or work . . . Every
morning, as you awaken, all discomforts, caused or
aggravated by stress and tension . . . will be noticeably
better or gone completely.*

*In a moment, you are going to drain all the liquid out
. . . Imagine now, there are tiny valves on the ends of
your fingers and toes . . . the valves are open now . . .
and you're letting the warm, orange liquid drain out
. . . As the warm liquid drains from your body and
mind . . . a pleasant feeling moves from your head to
your toes . . . your body and mind are being relieved
of all the negativity . . . all the restrictions . . . all the
limitations you've been carrying around for so long . . .
Just imagine them flowing out of you with the liquid
now . . . Just imagine you can see it . . . and you can . . .
feel the warm liquid leaving you now . . . as the last*

drop of liquid drains, you get a feeling of lightness . . .
a feeling you've released a lot of the negativity you've
been harbouring within you for so long . . . By the end
of this day . . . definitely by tomorrow . . . you will have
noticed a difference . . . positive little changes in your
attitude . . . Your opinion of yourself will have improved
. . . You are going to feel more confident . . . you are
going to be more confident . . . and it is going to show
. . . You are going to feel free and at ease with those
you associate with at home or work . . . Day by day,
there will be a slow, steady release of all the negativity
you've been experiencing . . . the negative feelings . . .
the negative actions . . . the negative thoughts you've
accumulated over the years . . . thoughts, from others,
that you've accepted about yourself . . . and began
thinking were true . . . even though they were not . . .
you have, within you, the ability and power to solve
every problem in your life.

In the past, you may have felt some problems were
beyond your abilities to solve . . . this is no longer so . . .
You now look upon all problems as opportunities to
expand your awareness . . . to develop your mind . . . to
discipline your thoughts . . . to achieve better control
of your actions. These abilities are within you but they
haven't been used effectively in the past . . . All of that
is changing now . . . You are now aware they exist and
you will soon find yourself using them every day . . .
Each time you think of the warm, orange liquid, more
of the restrictions and limitations will be released . . .
You'll be able to work with it yourself . . . you are going
to get all the negative thoughts out of your life . . . they

no longer exist unless you let them exist . . . they are no longer valid.

Continue to relax now and listen . . . In a moment, I will count from ten to one . . . At the count of one, let your eyes open . . . and you will again be fully alert, rested and refreshed . . . filled with abundant energy . . . For the remainder of the day, you may experience a pleasant feeling of inner-warmth as a result of your improved circulation . . . ten, nine, eight . . . coming up now . . . seven, six, five . . . more and more aware . . . four, three, two, one . . . eyes open.

· · · · · · · · · · · · · ·

Deepening your hypnosis

Once you have become accustomed to using the Progressive Relaxation induction to relax your body physically and/or the Orange Liquid as a mind clean-out of negative doubts and fears, you may want to look at the following exercises for attaining deeper hypnosis. It is important to note that, as you practise self-hypnosis regularly, you will find it easier to go deeper much more quickly. These exercises will help you train your mind into becoming even more relaxed. As with the Progressive Relaxation induction, these scripts have been tried and tested for maximum effectiveness. You will need to record these 'deepeners' or learn them precisely.

Imaginary arm lift

Sit in a comfortable chair with armrests for your arms. Close your eyes and take some deep breaths. Take a minute or two to focus on your breathing and help you relax or you can listen to the Progressive Relaxation induction with these words added to the end.

In a few moments you can take some time to work with your imagination and focus . . . When you have concluded this exercise . . . you will be able to count yourself out of hypnosis . . . slowly and rhythmically from ten to one. At the count of one you will open your eyes and feel very comfortable . . . and happy with yourself . . . that you have taken the time to practise with your mind . . . allowing you to deepen your self-hypnosis.

Now allow your body to relax as you focus on your breathing. Then after taking about five breaths, start to bring your attention to one of your arms, keep your arms on the chair as you imagine one of your arms is beginning to slowly lift up. But not your . . . 'actual' . . . arm, but your shadow or imaginary arm . . . lifting up . . . Imagine in your mind's eye you can see it moving slowly . . . It may take some time or it may not . . .

[Pause for 30 seconds.]

Now concentrate . . . and focus on your arm . . . and without lifting you real arm . . . imagine that the shadow of your arm or pretend arm is wanting to move up . . . up about 10cm (3 inches) above the arm of the chair . . . imagine that without your 'real' arm moving

*a sort of shadow of your arm . . . your pretend arm . . .
starts to move . . . a little at first . . . it moves very
slowly . . . allow your imagination to see your pretend
arm moving comfortably and slowly . . . up and up
so it eventually becomes straight . . . out . . .and level
with your shoulder . . . It may happen straight away
or it may take some time while you concentrate . . .
it is your imagination so you can start to visualize . . .
imagine . . . and see in your mind's eye . . . your shadow
arm moving . . .The more you concentrate and focus
the easier it becomes . . . take a few moments to
watch your pretend arm move . . .* [leave 1 minute's
silence in the recording to allow yourself to focus on
this exercise]. *Now you can let your arm go back and
join your real arm on the chair . . . now you can count
yourself out of hypnosis . . . slowly and comfortably
from ten to one and then open your eyes.*

Ruler deepener

*What I would like you to do is imagine a 1m (3ft) ruler
in front of you. This ruler is a very special ruler . . .
because it measures relaxation. See the ruler in your
mind's eye . . . What colour is it?*

*Now if you look more closely . . . you will see there
are numbers on this ruler . . . what colour are the
numbers . . . At the very top . . . you can see a number
one . . . and at the bottom you can see the number 100.*

*In a few moments a number will appear more clearly
as you look down the ruler. . . this number will be your*

level of relaxation. Now drag your eyes very slowly down the ruler until you see a number show up more than the others. Notice what the number is . . . This is the number of your current relaxation . . . now drag your eyes even more slowly down . . . down to a number further down . . . and as you do . . . feel yourself going deeper and deeper into relaxation . . . as you drag your eyes down another number shows up more than the rest even further down . . . remember there is no hurry . . . [a long pause here] *. . . feel yourself being gently pulled into a wonderful deep relaxation . . .* [do this until you reach 100 and then come back up] *. . . Now take a deep breath . . . practise this several times and every time I ask you to do this . . . you will eventually find that you go even deeper . . . than you are now. Take another deep breath . . . breathe in . . . now breathe out.*

What is truly amazing about this ruler is that you can actually determine your own relaxation . . . by picking a number . . . and going straight there . . . Now look at the ruler . . . and go up to number 5 . . . now slowly drag your eyes down to number 15 . . . now in your own time slowly drag your eyes down to number 50 . . . and this may take a little longer but . . . in your own time . . . go down the ruler to 75 . . . and finally drag your eyes . . . ever so slowly to 90 . . . You can now allow yourself to pick your own level of relaxation.

As you sit there enjoying the feeling of relaxation . . . and allowing yourself to go easily and effortlessly into rest . . . visualize yourself in a place that you have enjoyed visiting . . . where you have felt happy . . .

calm . . . and relaxed . . . Take your time and when you are ready open your eyes.

. . . .

Procedures for 'deepening' your hypnosis

You can suggest to yourself that your relaxation is becoming deeper and deeper. You can say, 'With each breath you take you go deeper and deeper.' You can also add, 'Your breathing is getting slower and deeper and more regular with every breath you take.'

Then allow periods of silence (a few seconds) in order to allow spontaneous deepening. You will notice that many of the suggestions already use the words deeper and deeper. However, you can add these deepeners to your own suggestions to deepen your hypnosis even more. Note that the deep sleep at the end of this deepener is optional and can be played as you are in bed ready to go to sleep, or just put the count out at the end of your audio.

Lift deepener

You will have to judge how much extra time to leave as a pause on this recording, as you want to give time for the lift to reach the different floors as you go through the process.

Imagine a lift . . . a very attractive lift . . . The doors open and you walk in . . . look around . . . it is a very special lift . . . You notice a panel with A, B, C . . . and BB displayed on it . . . You realize that BB is the basement of your relaxation . . . You press 'A' and the doors close . . . and

*the lift descends . . . as it goes down . . . down . . .
you feel a wonderful sensation of very, very . . . deep
relaxation . . . say to yourself 'A' when you get to
floor 'A' and the elevator stops moving . . . you say
to yourself 'A' . . . as the doors begin to open . . . but
before you notice they open very far . . . you press
the letter 'B' on the panel . . . and watch the lift doors
close . . . As you feel the lift going gently down . . .
down . . . down . . . all the way down to the next
floor . . . when it reaches that floor say to yourself 'B' . . .
The lift doors begin to open, but again . . . before they
do . . . and because you know you can go deeper . . .
press the letter 'C' . . . and the lift starts to slowly . . . go
drifting . . . floating . . . down . . . all the way down . . .
to floor 'C' . . . As you reach this floor you say 'C' to
yourself . . . the lift doors start to open . . . but you
do not wait . . . because you want to go down to the
basement of relaxation.*

*So look again at the panel and press the letters 'BB' . . .
the lift starts to descend . . . slowly and comfortably . . .
allowing you to drift deeper . . . deeper . . . deeper
down . . . to the very basement of your relaxation.
Down . . . down . . . now you will be soon at the
basement of your relaxation . . . So relaxed . . . so . . .
calm . . . so free. And when you get to the basement
say 'BB' . . . The doors open to a very comfortable
room and you notice in the room is a very comfortable
large couch . . . you decide to go over and sit on the
couch . . . you realize this is your special place . . . where
you can relax so deeply . . . so comfortably . . . and
allow some time to enjoy the relaxation.*

*Now it is time to count yourself out of hypnosis or just
allow yourself to go into a wonderful deep sleep.*

Further suggestions

Here are a few suggestions that you can use to start training
yourself in self-hypnosis. They are very general and will be
perfect to help you practise getting into the trance state.
Once you are familiar with the process you can choose an
appropriate suggestion for a specific problem or issue you
want to work on. My favourite is the Ego suggestion as it
does not need to be altered and can be used by anyone.

Ego suggestion

*As you relax, more and more deeply . . . your own self-
healing forces are switched on . . . Muscles, nerves, the
very fibres of your being . . . rest and relax . . . Every
system slows down . . . So your whole being rests . . .
Healing forces check every part of you . . . Repairing,
replacing and re-energizing . . . Soothing your mind and
nerves . . . So, this relaxation enables you to feel fitter
and stronger in every way . . . Your nerves stronger
and steadier . . . Your mind serene and tranquil . . .
you experience peace of mind and a deep sense of
wellbeing . . . as you drift deeper and deeper . . .*

*These feelings stay with you long after you open your
eyes . . . You feel more self-confident . . . Your willpower,
determination and self-assurance grow and develop . . .
You feel more comfortable . . . within yourself and*

within your surroundings . . . Day by day these positive feelings develop inside you . . . Day by day, life becomes more enjoyable . . . more fulfilling . . . You feel so much better . . . within yourself . . . and about yourself in every way.

The way your subconscious now protects you is to allow you to be more relaxed . . . and calm . . . and easy . . . and comfortable. You discover . . . because you feel so comfortable . . . that you enjoy life much more . . . Your reactions are mature and natural . . . These changes occur because your subconscious mind wishes to take care of you as well as possible . . . Your subconscious recognizes your need to feel secure . . . and to be able to look ahead with confidence and optimism.

When you experience hypnosis again you will find yourself returning quickly and easily to an even deeper level of relaxation . . . even more relaxed than you are now . . . In a few moments I will count from ten to one and on the count of one you will be fully awake, fully aware and your eyes will open . . . ten, nine, eight coming up now . . . seven, six, five . . . more and more aware . . . four, three, two, one . . . Eyes open, feeling good about yourself.

Assertiveness (to be yourself)

You know the key to success and enjoyment in your life is assertiveness . . . Because you want to be assertive, you are not afraid to ask for help when you need help . . . You are not worried about offering constructive criticism to your colleagues and friends . . . You can refuse to do a favour for your friends and relatives if you do not wish to do so . . . When your boss or someone else shouts at you or is rude to you . . . you can tell them that you resent their behaviour if the time is appropriate.

You feel good about yourself for asserting your rights . . . You know you have the right to change your mind. Others will respect you because you are honest with them about your feelings . . . and you treat them with respect . . . You know that the world is not perfect . . . but others will be more likely to change if you change yourself . . . you find you like yourself . . . and feel good about yourself.

It is such a relief not having to put on a mask and suffer in silence . . . It is such a relief not having to pretend and lie . . . It feels so good to be able to be just yourself.

Because you can just be yourself you enjoy your relationships more . . . The barriers between yourself and others are removed . . . You really get to know others and others get to know who you are . . . You feel a bond with other people and the world and you find out that your timing is excellent to speak your mind.

Sleep

You find you sleep soundly and peacefully for the length of time that you require . . . your dreams are pleasant.

You can imagine yourself calm and relaxed and comfortable . . . relaxing deeply with each breath . . . You picture yourself asleep and your chest moving up and down . . . As soon as you close your eyes when you put your head on the pillow . . . you feel drowsy and slip into sleep very quickly.

If you want to mull over the day's events before you go to sleep the time will seem to pass far more quickly than usual . . . and you find ways to put this time to constructive use . . . The sleep you have is so deep and relaxing that you awake at the correct time . . . refreshed and relaxed and ready to begin a new day . . . When you have less time than usual to sleep . . . the sleep you have is more effective . . . Every hour seems like two hours and you wake refreshed.

You sleep soundly and peacefully for the time required . . . and you are drowsy and relaxed as soon as you put your head down on your pillow and fall asleep quickly.

After you've practised going into hypnosis a few times, you'll probably find the process gets easier. Your body and mind will quickly get used to going into a relaxed state and you may notice yourself going a little deeper each time. A lot depends upon circumstances and everyone is different, so no two experiences are the same. One thing is for sure: regular self-hypnosis sessions are hugely beneficial both physically and mentally. If you want to train your mind to relax and 'let go' it just takes practice, and the next chapter is all about developing that skill.

RECAP ✍️

* Use the Progressive Relaxation induction script to get familiar with being in hypnosis.

* Remember the checklist before you start your self-hypnosis session so you are totally prepared.

* Once you become familiar with being in hypnosis you can try some 'deepeners' to achieve a deeper trance state.

* The Orange Liquid suggestion is a great de-stress tool or alternative induction.

* Try using some of the example suggestions to become more familiar with self-hypnosis.

* Like any activity, the more you practise the better you become. The more times you go into hypnosis the easier it becomes. Practise it daily for at least three weeks to form your new 'self-hypnosis' habit.

Chapter 5

Exercises for focus and depth

*'Thought is useful when it motivates for action,
and a hindrance when it substitutes for action.'*

BILL RAEDER

There are some useful, simple but effective exercises to practise and deepen your hypnosis just by increasing your concentration and focus. The more you practise the easier it will be to achieve a deeper hypnotic trance. In this chapter you'll find a selection of traditional exercises that have been proven to work for decades, with some dating back to the early 1920s, and are part of the history of hypnosis.

I suggest you avoid using your own words at first as these exercises have been proven to work exactly as they are presented here. The reason for this is because if you decide to add words to the inductions you may just stop the process from working at all. I also recommend you wait before you add suggestions at the end of the induction exercises as the object is to focus on your depth of trance, which in the end will help the overall effectiveness of self-hypnosis.

When you've practised the exercises several times and become familiar with them, you can then begin to add 'suggestions' at the end. You should wait until you are skilled in achieving a deeper trance and have studied the chapter on how to create suggestions. Some people may take shortcuts around these types of exercises and so miss out on the very important extra practice they could benefit from, but in the longer term the effort really does pay off.

The more you practise the techniques to relax and focus, the more effective your self-hypnosis sessions will become.

For these basic exercises, you can either sit in a comfortable chair or lie on a bed and fix your eyes on a spot or a mark on the wall or ceiling. If you are sitting down, a crystal ball or an object like a shiny stone or a crystal is ideal.

At the turn of the century, hypnotists used an old-fashioned pocket fob watch to induce their clients, which worked very well. The watch was generally shiny and made of gold or silver, and the hypnotist would swing it from side to side in front of the subject's eyes so that they focused on both the sparkle and the rhythmic movement, as the watch was swinging. While this was happening, the hypnotist would repeat instructions for them to become tired and sleepy and further instructions to deepen their trance. Since you are working without a hypnotist you'll have to use your focus and concentration to take you into the trance state.

It isn't that we lack the power to make suggestions to ourselves – most of us are very good at accepting negative damaging suggestions from others and ourselves – but often we lack the knowledge of how to employ this power of self-suggestion positively because of our own self-induced limitations.

Tips for practising self-hypnosis

The first general relaxation may take some time and have to be repeated a number of times, but later the trance state, or an increased state of suggestibility, can be created fairly quickly without the routine of relaxation.

To get the most successful trance there are some important steps, such as following the checklist of instructions in Chapter 4 (*see page 44*) and, more importantly, by reading more about hypnosis throughout the book, in order to boost your self-belief that you can do it and that it is a perfectly natural ability, although rarely used. Reading through all the chapters will prevent you from having to struggle by not knowing what you really should be experiencing. Remember, everyone experiences hypnosis differently so don't waste your energy worrying whether or not you are hypnotized, just go with the experience. As the highly respected John Watkins recommends:

> '*You should model the hypnotist by talking slowly with a soft voice... the state of relaxation... you can repeat the words to yourself, calm, easy, comfortable, let yourself go; let the muscles loose, all your body relax; it's all through you.*'

There are a huge variety of ways to hypnotize yourself that you can use without recording a script but I have chosen some of the most effective and easiest-to-achieve methods.

The exercises below were not designed to be rushed and should, in fact, be done rather slowly and comfortably. They are excellent training for getting used to relaxing the body and hypnotizing yourself.

Make sure you test each method, as some work better for one person while somone else may prefer an alternative. By experimenting you will see which is more helpful to you personally.

Breathing method

Some people, if they are well versed in meditation or deep-relaxation techniques, may want to use their breathing as a method of inducing trance.

First close your eyes and start to think about your breathing. Regulate your breathing to be rhythmic, with comfortably slow and deep long breaths so you are comfortable. Focus on each breath, thinking about what it is doing and imagining how your chest is moving up and down. As you do this you can start to let go of all your everyday thoughts, replacing them with focusing on your breathing.

Then just think about your muscles, from your feet up or from your head down, as a short version of the Progressive Relaxation induction (see page 51), which you can do casually from memory. Let each muscle relax and go limp whilst still being aware of your breathing.

This exercise can last as long as you like and you can even use it to send yourself off to sleep, but even just a few minutes of this concentrated relaxation each day is excellent for your general health.

Coin induction

Lie down and close your eyes. Place a coin on the space between your eyebrows. Close your eyes and now look up, still keeping your eyes closed. Look up as if you are looking at the spot between your eyebrows. Keep looking up until it feels uncomfortable, and then relax your eyes. Don't think about them. Just let them do what they want to do.

If you use this method daily for a couple of weeks you will generally find you can go into relaxation much more quickly.

Eye fixation

Lie down and think about your body relaxing, then find a spot on the ceiling. Don't stare at it but just focus on the spot. Don't try to do or think about anything else and when it becomes an effort to keep your eyes open, let them close. The object of this relaxation exercise is to let your mind and body gradually slow down.

Gaze steadily at the spot. Let the image of what you are looking at register in your mind while continually looking at it. Ignore any other ideas or sensations that may pop into your mind, such as noises or breathing.

If your mind starts to wander, bring it back to focusing on the spot. As you do this, at some point you will start to feel tired, especially in your arms, hands, shoulders, legs and feet. Start to think how each muscle 'feels', going through each muscle one at a time, travelling down your body.

Take your attention to your right hand and keep your attention there for about 15 seconds, then bring your attention to your left hand for 15 seconds. Then go to each muscle in turn and focus on it for about 15 seconds. You will notice that when you think of one body part the others will be forgotten. Go over the main muscles in your body – your feet, legs, stomach, chest, arms and shoulders – three times, for 15 seconds each. You will begin to notice that tensions that may have been present will no longer be there.

Start to concentrate on your bodily functions such as your breathing. Think about your breathing and listen to it. Focus on your breath and make it become even, more rhythmic and regular. Now start to count your breaths while keeping your breathing regular and easy.

Take a few moments just to close your eyes and focus on your breathing. Notice how it feels that with every breath you take you can become more and more relaxed.

Crystal ball

For this exercise you'll need a crystal ball (these are widely available to purchase and fairly inexpensive); alternatively you could use a quartz crystal, a glass of water or a mirror.

Place the crystal ball on a stand and stare at it with your eyes half closed. Let yourself become aware of your body and that it may be becoming heavier and that you are becoming drowsier and your eyes feel as though they want to close. When it becomes too much of an effort to keep your eyes open you can let them close. You can then clear your mind and keep it clear. Thoughts may drift into your mind but gently push them away and continue to rest and become drowsier. You cannot have two conflicting thoughts at one time, so it is your responsibility to push away any negative or interrupting thoughts.

Counting into hypnosis

At the word 'one' allow your eyes to close. 'Two' and slowly open them, 'three' close them and 'four' open them again. Continue counting and allowing your eyes to gently close on the odd numbers and open on the even ones.

Do it comfortably and easily, make the suggestion to yourself that your eyes are becoming heavier and heavier and before you have been counting for very long they will be so heavy that it will be too much of an effort to open them. Continue counting until this occurs and then you can start your 'main' suggestions.

Use your sensations to induce hypnosis

If you have any sort of arm injury, I don't recommend trying this exercise.

Lie on the bed or the floor with your arms resting by your sides. When you feel relaxed after about 10 seconds, raise your right arm about 15cm (6 inches) above the bed (or floor) and let your fingers stretch out very straight. Let your arm become stiff and straight. Notice your other arm is limp and relaxed at your side. Keep still and focus on your stiff arm, notice how it feels as you keep it stiff. Notice the different tensions in this arm from the rest of your body.

Now turn your attention to your limp relaxed arm and notice the different feelings in each. Switch from one to the other slowly and purposely.

Now begin to increase the sensations in your right arm. Hold it tense for about 10 seconds or until it feels uncomfortable, then let it gently drop down and feel the relief of the relaxation and notice how it feels, and the sensations in this arm. Now repeat this procedure with your left arm. Then rest and repeat the procedure about three times. In the resting period say the words, 'relax even more, my arm is becoming more relaxed'.

Arm levitation

While lying relaxed, without altering the position of your body raise your right arm until, with fingers stretched straight out, the arm is raised about 15cm (6 inches) off the couch or floor where you are lying. Make sure it is extended stiff and straight, while the left arm remains limp at your side.

Make sure that you don't move your body or limbs and, apart from the muscles involved in raising your arm, you are completely relaxed. While the arm is extended, mentally note the different sensations for tension in this arm from those in the rest of the body. Switch your attention to the tense arm and then to the limp one and counteract the sensation in each.

When you plainly notice that the feeling of the relaxed state of your body is different from the tenseness of your arm, start to increase this difference in sensation by intensifying the tension in the right arm by tensing the muscles. Keep them tense for about 2–5 seconds, but when this becomes slightly painful let the arm go limp and drop. Then concentrate on your body going deeply relaxed as if it is sinking more deeply into the mattress, cushions or whatever you are lying on.

Imagination induction

You can use the garden bench from the Progressive Relaxation induction (*see page 51*) by thinking about it and imagining you are there again, just as you were when you were listening to the audio recording.

As you are sitting comfortably you see a little way ahead ten steps that lead to a lower part of the garden . . . and you can see just a few feet in front of the bottom step a large heavy wooden door . . . set in an archway made out of stone that leads to another part of the garden . . . you don't know what it is like through the door but you have this feeling that it is a wonderful peaceful place, a special place for you . . . you feel the need to explore and so you decide to walk down the steps . . . you know instinctively that each step will bring a feeling of deep relaxation . . . you walk over to the top steps and you begin to descend. On the first step a wonderful feeling of relaxation comes over you . . . on the next step you feel you are going deeper and deeper into relaxation . . . down . . . to the third step, even deeper relaxed . . . the fourth step, deeper still . . . down to the fifth . . . the sixth . . . and the seventh . . . feeling deeper and deeper relaxed . . . you are nearly at the bottom now . . . the eighth step you are feeling so, so, relaxed . . . the ninth and the tenth . . . you begin to walk over to the doorway knowing that on the other side is the most beautiful place . . . your special place . . . as you put your hand on the large handle the door creaks open and you are confronted with the most beautiful view.

What makes this place so special is that you can add or take away whatever you like, whether it be mountains, sand or flowers . . . you look around and you design your special place . . . you know that this is the basement of your relaxation and that you can come here at any time . . . to address your subconscious or just to relax . . . You see a comfortable place to sit. You can even lie down if you wish . . . You walk over and make yourself comfortable and as you do . . . a feeling of pure peace of mind and a deep relaxation washes over you like a wave and both in your body and mind you are in complete harmony . . . totally relaxed . . . as you relax your mind it re-energizes itself, your body allowing your own healing forces to function.

Once you have established a good relaxed state of hypnosis, you can then add your suggestion, or even a deepener from Chapter 5 to further increase the depth of your trance. Or if you wish, just enjoy a wonderful, peaceful mind quietness. In the next chapter you'll learn how to create a suggestion and what makes it powerful or ineffective just by changing a few words. It contains key information to help you personalize your suggestions and not just rely on generic scripts.

RECAP

- If you use the exercises in this chapter you'll find the depth of your hypnosis will increase. The more you repeat them, the deeper you'll go.

- Don't worry about whether you think you are hypnotized or not as everyone experiences hypnosis differently. Just go with the experience and allow yourself to relax naturally.

- As you practise you'll probably find it easier to focus, both in and out of hypnosis. This is the benefit of a quieter mind.

- Control your own mind: you cannot have two conflicting thoughts at one time so it is your responsibility to push away any negative or interrupting thoughts by thinking about happy experiences or wishes.

Chapter 6
Formulating suggestions

*'A man is but the product of his thoughts:
what he thinks, he becomes.'*
MAHATMA GANDHI

Once you have mastered hypnotizing yourself then it is time for you to choose or create your own personal suggestions, because when you are in a hypnotic state you are more open to your positive suggestions. In hypnotic language, the word suggestion is either a command or an instruction to the inner mind; for example, an idea or plan put forward for consideration.

Hyp-notes

Émile Coué the founder of self-hypnosis, explained that if you believe you can do a certain thing, providing it is possible, you will be able to do it, however difficult it may be. Whereas if you *imagine* that you *can't* do the simplest thing, it is impossible for you to do it – molehills become mountains – logic has little to do with it, neither has someone's 'will', as with a fear of heights, for example.

Your mind is much more receptive to suggestions when in a state of hypnosis. More things are perceived to be possible without the conscious mind interfering, and inhibitions and limitations are reduced. The words you use in your suggestions in hypnosis are very powerful and to be able to formulate them correctly, you need to understand some basic principles. As Derek Forrest, professor of psychology and author of *Hypnotism: A History*, explains, in the hypnotic state, attention is not subject to any self-regulatory control but it can be influenced by suggestion from within.

What is a suggestion script?

A suggestion script is a text of specially formulated words designed to bring about the changes you would like. It can be tailor-made to your own requirements, and I've included a range of script suggestions in the following chapters, which deal with both common and not so common issues. For example, the 'Stop smoking' script in Chapter 9 (*see page 165*) has remained virtually unchanged since I introduced the method in 1989, and many of the scripts used today are from the early 1900s. There hasn't been anything 'new' in hypnosis since the turn of the century, just different ways to present and explain it, because the basics are still the same.

Before creating your suggestions

When dealing with the mind there are many variables at play and what works for one person may not work for another, so if, after some practice, you choose to create your own suggestions then here are some general guidelines and simple 'rules' to help you formulate your own tailor-made suggestion scripts. As a general principle: **the simpler the suggestion the better**.

It is not productive to expect the help of your subconscious, if you are making it impossible for a suggestion to work. For example, it is not such a good idea to expect to work very hard with long hours and then believe you would be able to go out on the town most of the time and have very little sleep, expecting to burn the candle at both ends. The subconscious is like a bank manager and it will only lend you energy if you can pay it back, in this case with rest.

If you are looking for an overall change rather than individual ones then as a first step write down your goals and analyse them. Structuring your suggestion to be detailed requires making a list of what you want to achieve.

Don't just say you want to succeed, write down the detail of how you plan to achieve your outcome and the precise nature of your goals. For example, how much money you wish to earn, or what size of business you require for you to attain your goal in life. Otherwise, the subconscious, being so literal, may just believe that keeping a roof over your head and food in the larder is successful, because you've neglected to explain how successful you want to be. Don't forget, your ideas of success are changing constantly as you mature and progress, so regularly review your plan and update your suggestions accordingly.

If you don't want your subconscious to act on out-of-date information, you need to reprogram it using your imagination and visualization. Just imagine if your idea of success as a child was just getting a job; then if you just said you wanted to be successful, that's all your subconscious would be programmed for. Consciously you may want riches but subconsciously you already have success if you have a job (which means any job), so it believes the instructions have already been carried out and no further work is done.

This is likely the reason why so many people stay in the same job or career, despite loathing it, year after year. More than likely they are giving themselves 'suggestions' that their mind is literally acting upon, keeping them in the same situation.

Case study

Alice, a 22-year-old web designer, came to see me for help with public speaking because she was due to give a presentation at work and couldn't face it. She'd had difficulty speaking to an audience for as long as she could remember; even at school she was almost paralysed if asked to stand up and speak. She lacked confidence and suffered low self-esteem and she was not even sure web design was something she wanted to do.

At the end of the session she told me that she could hear my voice on and off with echo-like sounds, but had no feeling in her body, as though she was floating, and her hands were tingling with electricity-like sensations, but she said it was very pleasant. She was very surprised at how relaxed she felt but also how 'empty' her mind had felt during the hypnosis.

Two weeks later Alice told me that her presentation had gone well and she was very pleased with herself. As a result, her confidence rocketed along with her self-esteem. She also made a major life change and decided to study interior design, as it was something she wanted to do. The power of the mind is just amazing.

Formulating a suggestion

There are some simple rules to follow when formulating your own tailor-made suggestions for writing powerful, life-changing suggestions. Here are the 'bullet points' to remember and below you will find more information about each rule:

❖ Use the present tense.

❖ Be positive.

❖ Be specific.

❖ Be detailed.

❖ Keep it simple.

❖ Use exciting and imaginative words.

❖ Affirm activity.

❖ Be accurate.

❖ Be realistic.

❖ Personalize it.

❖ Symbolize your suggestion.

❖ Be repetitive.

Use the present tense

Always suggest that you are already acting out the behaviour change by using the present tense (i.e. 'I am...' or 'I have...'), so you might say, for example,

❖ 'I am confident when...'

❖ 'I have the skills...'

- ❖ 'I maintain my...'

- ❖ 'I create a...'

Note: If you say, 'I will enjoy eating healthily', the subconscious could take this to mean sometime in the future – maybe 20 years from now!

The only exception to this rule is if you have a physical condition, such as a broken leg that you want to heal, when you should use a progressive form of the present tense, for example:

- ❖ 'My leg heals quickly and comfortably.' *Or,*

- ❖ 'My leg is healing quickly and comfortably.'

You might also want to add a time element, for example,

- ❖ 'My leg heals in half the time it would normally take.'

Direct suggestions for future behaviour should also be phrased in the present tense, for example:

- ❖ 'I always feel comfortable in company...'

- ❖ 'Day by day I feel more enthusiastic about...'

Be positive

Try to avoid using negative words (i.e. 'I don't...' or 'I won't...') in your suggestions. Don't mention what you are trying to change or avoid feeling. Create a positive mental picture of what you want to do, as if it has already happened, in order to move towards your goal. For example:

- ◆ 'I am more confident.' rather than 'I never feel self-conscious.'

- ◆ 'I am a good public speaker.' instead of 'I won't feel nervous when I speak in public.'

Be specific

Confine your suggestions to one issue or outcome, and don't try to cover a collection of problems all at once, at least to begin with. For example, don't tell yourself, 'I feel confident, I control my weight and I sleep soundly.' This could be counter-productive. It's like trying to carry far too much at once, to avoid making a return journey, but then dropping everything and so making more work for yourself. Try not to overload your subconscious with a selection of major problems.

Be detailed

As described in more detail earlier in the chapter, analyse your goal and structure your suggestion script to cover details of your desired change, behaviour or attitude. Don't just say you want to succeed – detail how, and what goals you would like to reach.

Keep it simple

Your subconscious needs to understand what outcome you want, so don't overcomplicate your suggestions. To do this, speak to your subconscious as though talking to a bright six-year-old child. Your subconscious is incredibly sophisticated but there is less chance of confusion when you keep the wording simple.

Use exciting and imaginative words

Make your suggestions full of feeling, excitement and energy. Use graphic, powerful words, such as:

❖ exciting

❖ wonderful

❖ dynamic

❖ vibrant

Affirm activity

Your suggestion should describe your action, not ability, for example:

❖ 'I exude confidence when I am at work' rather than, 'I am confident in the office.'

❖ 'I lose weight easily by controlling what I have to eat' instead of 'I can lose weight.'

Be accurate

Suggest the EXACT improvement and result you wish to achieve. Plan out the details. For example, if you have an illness or even something as simple as a cold, saying, 'I feel healthy' is not specific enough. So make sure you say what you want – within reason – such as,

❖ 'I am recovering rapidly and with each new day I feel better and better.'

❖ 'Every time I get up to speak I immediately feel completely relaxed.'

Be realistic

There are circumstances where it is wrong to suggest perfection. For example, saying 'I am happy all the time' would not be a realistic suggestion, and would probably be rejected by your subconscious. We all know there are times when we are not happy, when happiness would not be an appropriate response at all (for example upon hearing of the death of a friend), so trying to program your subconscious in this way will only be confusing.

Personalize it

Structure your suggestions for the change you want to see in yourself, your attitudes and your actions. You may not be happy with the behaviour of others, but the easiest way to initiate change in the people around you is to change yourself, so picture yourself as you want to be. Your suggestion should state the exact improvement you wish to achieve, for example:

+ 'I am calm and in control when speaking to my colleagues at work.'

+ 'I greet each person at family gatherings with cheerfulness.'

+ 'I make healthy choices when I am eating in restaurants.'

Symbolize your suggestion

Picture yourself as you want to be or having achieved your goal by building a detailed picture in your mind. Don't worry if it's exaggerated, as long as there is an element of possibility. Doing this type of visualization work gives you huge scope, as most dreams are possible if you are willing to work at them.

Be repetitive

❖ Use repetition in your suggestion while varying the words you use and including a broad range of convincing adjectives to describe it, so your suggestion is attractive, a little like selling a product. The more often you picture an idea (even in a slightly different way) the more of a possibility it becomes. For example:

❖ 'I feel calm and tranquil while working' *and*

❖ 'My mind is crystal clear when I concentrate' *and*

❖ 'I focus quickly and easily when faced with difficult situations.'

You can use the following words more often, as these are words that can be used as a bridge between the thoughts in the suggestion. They also help you go deeper into hypnosis:

❖ now

❖ down

❖ deeper

Additional guidelines

Using the above rules you can personalize one of the scripts included in this book to fit your individual needs. You may even decide to design a whole suggestion yourself. And, of course, you might choose to use the scripts just as they are.

If it is a sport you want to learn, before creating your suggestion you'll need information on what skills you need to acquire in order to play well. Self-hypnosis can then be used as a short cut to help you improve those specific skills. You can find out the details from an expert and then include this information in the suggestion script.

For example, many beginners learning tennis forget to keep looking at the ball when they hit it with the racquet and follow the racquet instead, so you could put some instructions in the suggestion that your eyes need to 'stay on the ball', then you will have created a new habit without the practice usually needed. You might say, for example, 'My eyes stay fixed on the ball until my racquet strikes it, which enables me to direct the ball exactly where I want it to go. My coordination is perfect, my arm movements strong and positive when directing my racquet to swipe the ball to its destination. I am fully confident in my coordination.' This would be a powerful choice of words and with a little adjustment could be used for a beginner at golf too.

It is generally accepted that the scripts for suggestions have to be long and repetitive. By accident I found this wasn't always necessarily so. When I developed the speed-reading technique, I found that a short, direct instruction was all that was necessary in some cases. You can start off with longer scripts, following the rules above, but as you get more confident with devising your own scripts, you may find that you're able to write more concise suggestions.

The English language is full of words that have more than one meaning, so think carefully before you give your instructions to your subconscious. Read and reread your suggestion before recording or memorizing it.

Each suggestion script provided in this book is carefully created to be a guide. You will be able to use the suggestion as it is, or introduce your own words to make it more tailor-made to your problem or you can even select paragraphs from each as a type of mix-and-match. Whatever you decide, you can be sure that even if you choose the 'wrong' suggestion all that will happen is that it simply won't work or your mind will edit out the unnecessary words and decide whether or not to activate the wanted ones. Minds are well protected from our inadequacies, so there is no need to worry whether you have it right or wrong.

Below you'll find two example scripts that, while excellent suggestions in their own right, could be used as the basis for creating a personalized script, using the guidelines above – once, of course, you have become more confident with using suggestions. You can tailor the tension relief script to specific situations that usually cause you stress. Character building is very subjective, and so this script can be amended depending upon the aspects of your character and personality you want to improve or reinforce.

Tension relief

As you breathe in slowly . . . you find that breath travelling all the way through your body, bringing a wave of relaxation that dissipates all the tension you have sensed for some time . . . tension that has interfered with the way you want to be . . . tension that has interfered with your work and enjoyment . . . from now on all that tension will be relaxed out of your body . . . leaving room for positive and happy thoughts . . . your subconscious will now find a constructive way of dealing with stress and tension . . .

Not all stress is negative stress . . . we need a certain amount of positive stress to encourage us to attain our goals . . . even to perform an act as simple as getting out of bed in the morning . . . now all your stress will be directed towards positive action . . . the remainder, which is just negative stress, will be breathed out of your body and disappear . . . actions or words that would have normally caused tension now give you a wonderful feeling of challenge . . . problems become obstacles to get round and your subconscious finds easy routes around such obstacles . . . your subconscious takes responsibility to handle all worries and problems in a positive way . . . leaving you free to enjoy your life . . . be successful at what you want to achieve . . . and let your body function correctly . . . no longer hampered by negative thoughts, your body and mind in harmony.

All doubts are replaced by a feeling of optimism . . . doubts are there to encourage you to look at all of your options . . . to help you take the correct decisions . . . not to prevent you from doing something you are capable of . . . now you trust your subconscious to channel stress and worries into the correct parts of your mind . . . keeping the positive thoughts and energy . . . and ridding you of the unwanted and damaging negative thoughts . . . while transferring the energy from these negative thoughts into constructive energy . . . energy is like electricity . . . it is neither good . . . nor bad . . . it just needs to be channelled in the correct area . . . to be constructive rather than destructive.

As this new formula for good health is activated, you feel better and better . . . more relaxed and calm . . . this in turn allows the healing forces of your body and mind to repair itself and replace negative thoughts and energize you with your natural regularity . . . you now look after your body and mind and treat them with the respect they deserve . . . and because of this you feel stronger and stronger to cope with everyday obstacles . . . so you now enjoy life even more.

Character building

Every trauma, problem and obstacle that has happened in the past has been put to use by building up your strength and your character . . . to allow you to begin to see your future more clearly . . . more positively than ever before . . . your emotions now begin to settle down . . . all the anger . . . the frustration and the hurt you felt before . . . and got in the way of your decision-making . . . are now back in their correct places . . . leaving valuable information . . . from experience . . . that will enable you to come to better and more constructive conclusions . . . the emotions settle down . . . no longer on the surface . . . no longer in the way of you thinking clearly.

They have served their purpose and because your mind is now stronger . . . clearer . . . and more positive than before . . . you begin to feel the benefits . . . your confidence is stronger and healthier . . . you believe in yourself as a person . . . you enjoy your new respect and no longer carry hurt around with you, like a damp bundle of dirty washing . . . instead you are proud of yourself and your new attitude . . . your attitude is no longer a problem.

You realize if people say hurtful things it is because it is they who have a problem . . . and are frustrated . . . with their problem . . . you can understand that the remarks and the actions . . . that would have hurt you in the past may be a retaliation . . . retaliation for a hurt they were experiencing . . . it does not prevent you from examining yourself to see if it is your fault . . . but this time you are able to do so in a constructive way . . . and you are able to work on your faults and weaknesses to enable you to grow and . . . be happy . . . and contented.

Your subconscious inner mind works at overcoming your weaknesses . . . the weaknesses that have caused you so much mental anguish . . . resulting in a wonderful peace of mind . . . as your emotions settle . . . new, positive emotions now come to the surface . . . replacing the old, useless, negative emotions.

. . . .

RECAP ✍

❖ By now you will understand the purpose of, and how to use, suggestion scripts in order to personalize them.

❖ Remember the simple rules for tailoring suggestions to achieve the outcomes and goals you desire.

❖ Be clear about your goals and outcomes for the suggestion. Write them down as a guideline and expand them using exciting language.

❖ When formulating your suggestions speak to your subconscious as though you were talking to a bright six-year-old using very easy to understand words or sentences.

❖ Go for what you want to achieve and instruct your subconscious according to your ultimate aims. However, be realistic – don't aim for a factual impossibility.

Chapter 7
Workplace stress

'A business like an automobile, has to be driven, in order to get results.'
B C FORBES

This chapter gives you some important pointers on how you can be much happier and more satisfied with your work. There will be signs to watch out for, especially if you tend to work too hard, and some useful scripts you can personalize to help you change your perspective for the better, giving you the chance to enjoy your life both at work, socially and at home.

Spending just a little time working on yourself and utilizing some specially designed stress-release suggestions in self-hypnosis can help keep your immune system strong and keep illnesses at bay. The alternative could be devastating so you need to set to work immediately on creating the strong new you, allowing you to work at your maximum potential whilst reducing stress, ultimately resulting in a satisfying, healthy and happy life.

There are many ways self-hypnosis can help in business:

❖ Job satisfaction

❖ Avoiding stress in the workplace

❖ Helping you get on with difficult bosses and colleagues

❖ Building self-confidence

❖ Changing your perspective and solving business difficulties

In particular, self-hypnosis can show its power in business in the all-important sales departments, and this chapter gives you some useful hints on how to maximize your productivity *without* stressing out.

Case study

When I was commissioned to use hypnosis to increase the time the telephone salespeople could spend selling on the phone, I was staggered by the success of just simple hypnosis suggestions. Within half a dozen sessions the general manager of the sales department said the time spent on the phone went through the roof. He had never seen anything like it in all his 20 years of experience of handling sales teams.

Unproductive mind viruses

Just as computer viruses can wreak havoc with technology, mind viruses can work silently within an organization, spreading and infecting the whole infrastructure. A mind virus is a change in behaviour caused by external stimuli, which is not always recognizable, as it is often accepted as 'normal' and not classed as 'negative'. Mind viruses can be negative thoughts and attitudes or physical and mental ailments. Stress, tiredness, anger or anxieties are just a few examples. Weight problems, excessive alcohol intake and smoking are subtler symptoms of problems in the workplace.

Stress is the natural reaction people have to excessive pressures, but if ignored it can lead to mental and physical ill health, resulting in absenteeism and lost productivity. It's also widely reported that stress can contribute to life-threatening issues such as type 2 diabetes, heart disease and strokes. These can be created by business pressures leading to an unhealthy lifestyle, such as eating unhealthy snacks in the office, being just too tired to eat healthy food or leaving no time for exercise.

The problem is that anyone can suffer from stress, depending on the circumstances they are in at the time, but they don't realize it until it has a strong hold on them, and according to the *Daily Mail*, a staggering 15 million days were lost in 2013 due to stress, anxiety or depression. Taking steps to prevent this, as either an employer or an employee, is good business. Even just one person can make a difference and that could be your input to helping make the workplace better by simply reducing your stress at work.

You can help yourself with self-hypnosis as a foundation for change. With its proven history of effectiveness, hypnosis is the most successful of any therapy to date for dealing with stress. It is the fastest, safest and most effective way to relax. You can do it yourself and its extra bonus is that it is free – it just takes a little time and effort.

Using self-hypnosis in the workplace can create
a happy and productive working atmosphere.

Scripts for reducing your stress at work

Here you'll find some work-related suggestions that you can record and play back to yourself. It really is that easy. Self-hypnosis is a great way to 'wind down' at the end of a busy day just before sleep. Once you get into the habit of doing it, you'll reap the untold benefits and realize your maximum potential.

Also, with the accessibility of smartphones, you can keep the recordings close to hand and use them whenever you feel the need, as well as using them at home. The advantage of self-hypnosis is that you can utilize it wherever you are. For example, if you are feeling a bit stressed, take some time out to listen to the Orange Liquid suggestion (*see page 57*) to relax yourself. If you need a quick 'boost' before an important meeting or public speaking you can use any one of the suggestions depending upon your personal circumstances.

Case study

When I had my hypnotherapy business there was a time when there were quite serious problems in the office. I worked from my home most of the time and I noticed a difference in the atmosphere when I arrived at the office. I suggested that since we were a training company teaching hypnotherapists to handle clients' stress we should use some group suggestion hypnosis. Everyone agreed and I created a suggestion for our employees that included everyone, even my business partner. We were all surprised and delighted at the result – it was amazing how it released the tension and how much more pleasant the working atmosphere became. A real case of practise what you teach.

Switching off

Nowadays people don't realize how much they use their mobile phones, as it has become a new habit. You just need to look around a restaurant or at any social occasion to see people constantly texting and checking their phones. I even see people using their phones while they are eating and they are oblivious to the fact that it is unhealthy. Most people are on their phones flicking from one app to the next, checking messages and looking at social media. The mind is constantly working like an overused computer, which may eventually cause it to break down. This multi-tasking is causing our brains to work differently and is even said to cause the brain's thinking and emotional matter to decrease, resulting in a reduced cognitive control.[10]

For some people just the thought of putting their phone or tablet on 'aircraft' or 'do not disturb' mode brings them out in a cold sweat, in much the same way as a phobia or anxiety attack would affect them, as it has to be a 'conscious' decision to do it. However, using self-hypnosis, you can easily help to form new habits focused on the use of technology. It happens as an automatic reflex like someone who no longer smokes not wanting a cigarette any more. Behaviour is subtly changed and you become not quite so reliant on checking your devices as frequently as before.

The result is that the brain has a rest from the constant bombardment of information and 'thinking', leading to a much calmer state, which in turn positively affects your general health and wellbeing. Productivity increases with a clearer mind and you benefit personally and professionally. You can design your suggestion around the times you want to be free. The key is to set workable boundaries for when it is acceptable to check your device. The rest of the time – such as mealtimes, social occasions, family time or just time for relaxation – can be 'device-free'. Below is an example you can use as the basis for your suggestion and you can add or subtract the parts that don't apply to you.

Constant checking of work

What a relief that everything is properly done! . . . you have finished all the work . . . you are so relieved now . . . nothing bothers you any more . . . you have no more need to worry . . . you have finished checking your emails, news and social media and all your usual websites . . . You have finished texting and now it is time for you to switch off . . . stop checking and working on your gadgets . . . just take a break . . .

You have decided to set aside working on your gadgets and checking them . . . you realize the world is not going to be changed because you are constantly on tap . . . that would only be for servants and slaves in the old days . . . You no longer want to be a slave . . . without a life ... get a life now ... start to live ... You start by creating a way to let your friends and family know ... that you will only be able to respond to them (unless there is an emergency) at certain times ... You have decided to do an experiment with your time ... and appreciate their help ... by understanding that you are not responding ... to their emails and texting ... at certain times ... so you can see how your concentration improves ... You find it easy to persuade them to work with you ... to be interested in the outcome ... as you know that they would secretly like to do this ... You know your friends will be looking forward to hearing from you ... but they know that it will be only at certain times ... you have told them of these times and you are delighted you are going to keep to them ... with this new healthy habit ... no need to keep checking your gadgets for mail or texts ... you don't need to worry ... about your friends or work.

You are now relieved as you realize that if you keep checking ... you will just be making unnecessary work for yourself ... it is futile to waste time ... continually checking.

You are realizing what you can do with the extra valuable time you used to spend checking ... you can read a novel ... go for a walk ... chat comfortably with friends without the constant worry of checking your messages or texts ... have a sound sleep ... what a wonderful life without constantly checking ... no more, now you can enjoy your work ... you are now free from the doubts and fears and look forward to having some well-deserved freedom.

General work-related suggestions

Here is where self-hypnosis comes in with a well-formed suggestion, and you will have the confidence and energy to go for what you want. The following scripts are general work-related suggestions that you can use depending upon your own situation. In addition to this list, you can use the 'Assertiveness (to be yourself)' script (*see page 71*).

Money

Day by day you observe how quickly and easily your finances . . . grow and grow . . . You allow money to come into your life . . . accepting all the gifts . . . the universe wishes you to have . . . You are happy accepting money . . . as money is an enabler . . . and you now want money in your life.

Because you would like to be financially secure . . . you feel a real satisfaction . . . knowing that you have enough money . . . to pay easily . . . for all those things you want to do . . . and to have . . . You enjoy doing . . . and having these things . . . You will find that you have less . . . and less . . . financial stress . . . and you feel good . . . as money just flows into your life . . . continually and easily . . . day by day . . . as you start to find new ideas that come to you about how you can make money in ways you enjoy . . . probably things you had not thought of before . . . as your subconscious works to attain your goals.

You enjoy this feeling of plenty and enjoy whatever positive things you wish to do with this income because it gives you freedom and you like being free to fulfil your heart's desires and attain your goals.

Now picture yourself as you want to be . . . Financially secure with an income that increases to a good level for you – a comfortable level . . . You enjoy living with this comfortable level of income . . . you like how you look . . . and what you can do with money . . .

You don't mind people seeing that your income has increased if and when you wish to . . . and the people around you will be happy for you.

You are very imaginative . . . and confident in your ability to succeed . . . Using your imagination to create a fountain of ideas . . . for easily achieving your goals . . . of making money.

To decide which of those many ideas to use . . . examine all the talents that you possess . . . against your perception of market opportunities . . . and decide which are the most appropriate . . . to achieve your first target with ease . . . It will form a building block . . . for the many future successes . . . of which you are capable.

Set that first target at a level which permits . . . ready and easy attainment . . . thereby measuring your confidence . . . in your natural talent . . . your ability to use it to achieve more ambitious goals.

Plan with great care . . . and rehearse with friends . . . or your colleagues . . . in your chosen venture . . . ensuring no detail is overlooked . . . in your quest for success.

Always keep in mind the likely future development of the market . . . or idea . . . that you choose to exploit . . . so that initial success leads inevitably . . . to many ever more satisfying ones . . . as the demand expands . . . for whatever product . . . or service . . . you are offering.

Remain flexible . . . since markets change frequently . . . and quickly as does technology . . . so adaptability . . . is your watchword . . . and the guarantee of your continuing success.

De-stress at work

Whatever you are doing wherever you are . . . you can take three breaths to relax . . . and induce the perfect state of calmness while still being alert.

Breathe in now and as you slowly breathe out say inwardly to yourself, 'calm . . .' Do that again and feel the wave of calmness wash over you . . . Once more . . . inwardly saying 'calm' to yourself as you breathe out – calm . . . calm . . . calm.

Whenever you do this . . . tensions and anxieties flow from you . . . leaving you feeling relaxed and perfectly in control.

And your mind knows that anytime you take these three calming breaths . . . your breathing will slow . . . your mind will clear . . . and you can continue whatever you are doing in a calm, positive, focused way.

*Use hypnosis to encourage your
imagination to create new ways to get
you out of difficult situations.*

Clearing negative emotions for work

*As you go deeper into relaxation . . . you feel all the
stresses . . . and strains . . . and fears . . . seeping away.
It is as if there is a stream . . . with clean . . . clean . . .
water . . . washing away the unpleasant feelings and
emotions that have been interrupting you throughout
your life . . . All the unnecessary fear that has caused
your restrictions . . . stopping you doing the things you
would like to do . . . or simply causing you discomfort
. . . all the negative thoughts that have prevented you
from enjoying your life . . . are being swept away . . .
Visualize your whole body and mind being relieved of
this debris . . . as it is swept out of your body and floats
away on your breath as you slowly and gently exhale.*

*Imagine that you are building up your immune
system and filling your stores of wellness as you
inhale . . . until your system is glowing with energy and
health . . . Your mind is extremely powerful and now
you are instructing it to take care of you . . . erasing all
the incorrect programs . . . that have plagued you for
so long.*

*Imagine a wonderful glow beginning to fill your
body, starting with your feet . . . this is your wellness
glow . . . feel it moving through your body as it
cleanses, repairs and heals . . . Feel how good your*

lower legs feel . . . and as the glow moves up your body . . . experience it healing as it flows through . . . experience your stomach . . . your back . . . your arms and hands . . . feeling so comfortable as the healing glow travels at a languid pace through your body . . . monitoring and healing. Your head . . . face . . . and scalp . . . feel so comfortable as the healing glow passes through . . . leaving your body comfortable and reinvigorated.

You know you can now access wellbeing through the power of your mind . . . this gives you a warm and comfortable feeling of confidence . . . Imagine a television set . . . project an image of yourself on the screen . . . you are healthy and happy . . . This is your blueprint for your mind, so if it needs working on to produce a healthier picture you can work on it now . . . You will notice there are dials on the television set . . . these dials are emotional dials that you can adjust to produce the picture you desire. There is a dial for good health. Look where the dial is showing . . . and then adjusted to excellent health . . . when you have the picture you are happy with . . . just allow the picture, and television, to fade away knowing that your blueprint for your inner mind is in place . . . you have set the program into action . . . as you drift into deep relaxation you tell yourself you are getting better . . . and better . . . day by day.

Fear of public speaking

Imagine yourself arriving at the venue you're going to speak at . . . you begin to feel more relaxed . . . It surprises you how very relaxed you begin to feel . . . In fact as you begin to see the people that you're going to talk to, you feel very comfortable and confident . . . your nerves become stronger and steadier . . . as your confidence begins to grow . . . you realize that talking to a crowd is only like talking to your friends . . . your friends don't always agree with you and you have to find interesting ways to sway their opinions . . . in fact you find it interesting to sway their opinions . . . just as you will when you speak to a crowd . . . you have all the skills you need to communicate naturally . . . and you find that as you realize this simple point . . . you become less and less conscious of yourself . . . and less preoccupied with yourself . . . you find that you are looking forward to speaking to a group . . . in fact any group . . . after all, they are people like yourself.

Imagine yourself at the end of the talk . . . or speech . . . and you are delighted to see the audience applauding . . . and happy . . . and smiling . . . you can tell they have enjoyed your talk and felt easy with your confidence . . . and easy manner . . . you were able to put your points across easily. Work on your picture, your dress rehearsal . . . until you are satisfied with the outcome . . . These are your instructions to your inner mind and you will find strategies to bring them into reality.

Increasing productivity

As you relax comfortably, calmly, and safely . . . you feel your confidence growing. With this comes an inner awareness . . . of your ability to increase productivity . . . your own and the team that you are part of . . . As any leftover stresses or doubts are dissolved away . . . you have renewed energy, enthusiasm and motivation . . . Every problem you encounter becomes an exciting challenge . . . that you can't wait to begin and complete. The more you achieve the easier it becomes . . . and the more confidence you enjoy . . . In your mind's eye you know exactly what you want to achieve . . . and you are now heading with ease towards that goal . . . You are clear in your thoughts . . . and you are always able to deliver.

Problem-solving whilst asleep

As you become adept at relaxing . . . you are able to rest fully and sleep well . . . always.

And when it is time for you to sleep . . . just spend a few moments scanning your body and mind for any tensions . . . Practise this now . . . and if you come across any anxieties, tensions, worries or fears . . . mentally massage them away . . . and feel soothed . . . sinking down into peaceful slumber . . . Every breath that you take relaxes you more and more while you drift away . . . As you sleep your mind is able to do its filing and organizing . . . and when you awaken, any problems that you had are sorted out . . . and you are aware of useful and workable solutions . . . Your dreams are creative and you awaken refreshed and keen to begin your day.

You can.

. . . .

RECAP ✍

* Self-hypnosis can be a huge help in most areas of business including productivity, better communication, sales and job satisfaction.

* Workplace stress contributes to illnesses such as heart disease, type 2 diabetes and strokes. Regular self-hypnosis is proven to help control stress and improve mental and physical health.

* Form a new habit of not checking your portable devices so much by using the 'Constant checking of work' script. You, and those around you, will notice the difference.

* Beware of 'mind viruses' in the workplace. Negativity can lead to an unhealthy work atmosphere.

* Use the specially designed scripts for work-related problems including fear of public speaking, money-related issues and tension relief.

* Remember you can use self-hypnosis 'on the go'. Simply record your suggestions onto a portable device and listen to them wherever you are, as long as you find a quiet place where you can be undisturbed.

Chapter 8
Perfect relationships

'Love is composed of a single soul inhabiting two bodies.'

ARISTOTLE

I gained my experience in relationship therapy quite by accident. I was single and had been offered the position of resident hypnotherapist in a luxurious five-star hotel in Langkawi in Malaysia. The position included a sumptuous hotel suite on the beachfront and all my meals. It was there that I planned to write my first book and I thought it would be the perfect place to meet a partner too. I felt I was in heaven, with incredible views from the hotel and a spectacular pool right in front of a wonderful private beach. But there was a drawback – I hadn't realized it was a honeymoon hotel, full of couples and people on their first or second honeymoon.

The sheer volume of couples I met, with many of them becoming clients, meant I was able to develop methods to help couples and singles with their relationship problems, but it also completely changed my life. In fact, using some of the techniques in this chapter, I was able to find my perfect partner, who is now my husband.

The perfect match

I have worked with couples who gave the impression that they were the perfect match and, to all their friends, they have an ideal life together. But everything isn't all that it seems, even to each other. I am not saying that there aren't people who have actually managed to get it right, who have a wonderful and balanced compatibility that leaves room for each of their personalities to grow separately, as well as growing closer together – but there aren't many who couldn't do with a little help to improve their relationships.

Often couples love each other yet live through conflict all of their lives, in a sort of love-hate relationship. If you take away the bickering and the hurt, there's little time for pleasure. The negativity is taking its toll in time and energy, but more often than not 'boredom' creeps into a long relationship and I've found it to be the most damaging.

However, if you decide to work at it, you can turn it round. My 'Blueprint For Love' suggestion (*see page 126*) has proven to be a great help, even for couples that believe their relationships to be OK. It is very useful to use this script if you are suspicious that there may be problems or boredom creeping into your relationship. It's also very good if you are single, in order to prepare yourself for when you do meet your ideal partner. It is an excellent mind detox and can be adjusted using the instructions on how to create your own suggestions in Chapter 6 (*see page 91*). However, it is important to make sure you don't make changes when you first use the script as it is tried and tested.

Improving your relationships

If you want to increase your opportunities of attracting a meaningful relationship or strengthening an existing one, then think of the self-hypnosis tools in this book as an opportunity to review all your behaviours and habits. Consider where you might be stuck or how reprogramming your behaviours could help you; for example, improving, your self-confidence or self-esteem in yourself and your body. Then you will give all your relationships a better chance of success.

Some people may be aware that they fall for the wrong partners and the pattern never seems to change. It is a learned program, activated through learned experience way back in the past. Wouldn't it be wonderful to change that program? Well, the good news is that you can. Although some very deep-seated issues may require the help of a hypnotherapist, you may be able to get to the source and work on it yourself with self-hypnosis. Whichever you choose, it can be fixed. In this chapter you will find some scripts especially for resolving this type of relationship issue.

For more general relationship issues, you'll quickly find that a good self-hypnosis suggestion can bring about amazing changes because often it is only a small but important change that is required. Maybe a change of attitude or even a simple change in behaviour is the only thing you need. Later on in this chapter I've included a few scripts about general relationship problems but of course you can design your own script to achieve your own aims.

Case study

Tony and Jane were both in their twenties. Tony was a creative person, a photographer, video producer and a creative designer. Jane was also very creative, but more negative in her approach to life. They listened to the Blueprint for Love audio every night for one week. The result was that the therapy allowed them to communicate more, to be able to talk to each other about the problems that were hindering the relationship. They had just come back together after a trial separation. After the half-hour self-hypnosis therapy sessions they definitely found a difference – a greater completeness, with a new understanding and ability to get things out into the open.

Jane told me, 'At the end of the week I felt very good. I had a new lease of energy, there was definitely a big improvement. I made two discoveries: things had to get worse before they could get better and we had to clear some things up so we could enjoy our relationship.'

With just a few sessions of self-hypnosis, it's possible to notice a shift in your relationship, as Tony and Jane did, and sometimes that's all it takes. When you are open to change, your mind takes on board all the suggestions and acts on them immediately. 'Couples therapy' using counselling or psychology alone can take years to bring about the sort of change that hypnosis can create in a very short time. If just a few self-hypnosis suggestions can make such a difference, imagine what you could achieve if you took more time. For instance, just a few minutes every day could ensure your relationship is regularly updated and kept in check or fine-tuned, as Rose and Alex in the following case study experienced.

Case study

Rose and Alex had no intention of having therapy as they said they already had a very satisfactory relationship, marred only by a lack of communication in certain areas. After talking to me they were mildly interested in having hypnosis to see if they would notice any changes. They didn't expect any but said they would be volunteers for my book, *Blueprint for Love,* and give it a try. Using the Progressive Relaxation induction (*see page 51*) to hypnotize them, followed by the 'Blueprint for Love' suggestion (*see page 126*), I hypnotized them together and used both the male and female suggestions. I didn't add any extra words for their particular problem and asked them to contact me a week later with some feedback.

Rose and Alex were both in their late fifties. Rose had been a nurse and Alex a businessman. Their attitudes towards my experiment were quite different. He was very sceptical but she was optimistic. She explained that Alex was the romantic, a perfect gentleman, but he listened to music she disliked, especially his choice of romantic songs. It made her feel silly as she was very practical, so she got impatient with him then felt bad about it. Also there were a couple of habits he had that really irritated her, otherwise everything was fine.

Rose called me a week after the self-hypnosis session to report there had been a definite shift in their relationship from her side. She found she was even playing the type of music Alex liked and was enjoying it. She not only felt very much more comfortable when he complimented her, but actually liked it. She also noticed a change when she went to a party during the week. She no longer felt she had to prove anything and had realized that her life was so much more content and happy.

Her attitude had changed and she saw the positive side of him and felt lucky to have such a wonderful caring man, instead of feeling threatened by him. Because of this new attitude, she felt they were communicating more and she was able to show her feelings – a new emotion, whereas before she realized this she thought she didn't deserve his compliments. When I asked her about his irritating habits she just didn't seem to know what I was talking about, then sheepishly laughed – proof that the annoying habits didn't bother her any more. I was surprised and delighted that self-hypnosis could have such a big impact after such a short time.

As I was writing about Rose a week later, Alex called me. He said he owed me an apology and said, 'If you had asked me earlier if there was any change, I would have said "no". However, with my workload yesterday I would have been, as usual, upset that my wife couldn't join me while I relaxed; she would be too busy in her own world. She never seemed to understand my need for company after a hard day. I would normally have to retire to my study alone to play my music on headphones. But since we saw you, I have to thank you. She not only asked me what I liked and how she could help, but actually played my favourite song when I arrived home; she said she could tell I was stressed. We now have a wonderful time. I've noticed Rose is more softer and feminine and it's great. I feel young again. I feel I have not only found a new wife but a new friend.' When I told him that a lot of couples resisted the necessity to improve their relationship because they thought it was great as it was, he agreed that he felt that way before, but not now and was delighted with the changes.

When Rose telephoned me a month later, I noticed that she was far more complimentary about Alex, sounding more like he was a new exciting relationship. When Alex called me, I found the same response. Both were like a pair of honeymooners! They sounded so happy that I felt all my research had been worth it. I found that the 'Blueprint for Love' suggestion has a positive impact whenever I use it. It also works extremely well with the hypnotherapists I have trained.

Attract the right relationships

You might also want to program your body to encourage an encounter of a magnificent kind. You don't have to be extremely confident even, but you must wish, and expect it to happen because it's amazing what positive energy and specific thoughts can achieve. For example, you must have heard people say things like, 'I was just thinking of buying a new sound system.' It's then as if the thoughts go into the universal Internet and get picked up by someone that has a sound system to sell. The person sending out the wish just thought it was coincidence. However, since there is now proof that telepathy works it shouldn't be so surprising. Nowadays, some people call it 'the Law of Attraction'. But, before you start making wishes you should take time to find out what you actually want in order to direct your mind to make your wishes come true.

When you know what you want in life then you can decide what type of partner to look for. You have to create a 'blueprint' outlining the qualities the people you want to attract will have. There are two important areas you can focus on, which can make a tremendous difference to the type of partners you attract.

1.   What you would like in a partner.

2.   Things you could share with them – activities or hobbies, music, friends etc.

Scripts for improving relationships

When you have used the Progressive Relaxation induction (*see page 51*) to experience hypnosis and feel comfortable with the relaxation you can use the Blueprint for Love below, as both an induction and a suggestion. There is a special part that can be added, if you are already in a relationship, otherwise it can be used for attracting a partner or making a current relationship even better.

> *'To love one's self is the beginning of a life-long romance.'* – OSCAR WILDE

Blueprint for Love (women) – for more satisfying relationships

Just allow yourself to relax and become comfortable where you are sitting or lying . . . Think about your feet . . . Notice what your feet are touching . . . now relax those feet and start to think about your breathing . . . Just allow it to become slow and rhythmic . . . and comfortable . . . in fact allow your whole body to relax.

Because you've recognized that you're now ready to make changes in your life . . . changes that alter the way that you experience the world . . . changes that enable you to see yourself in a more positive light . . . changes . . . so that you can truly enjoy your

*experiences . . . not only is it time to change the way
you perceive yourself . . . it's also time to free yourself
of the unhelpful labels . . . labels that may be associated
with some of the sensations that you feel . . . labels
that limit your enjoyment and prevent you from living
your life to the full . . . the words 'good' and 'bad' are
nothing more than labels . . . generally when we get
what we want, we call it 'good' . . . when we don't get
what we expect, we call it 'bad' . . . good and bad are
only labels because they merely reflect our perceptions
and our expectations.*

*Our perceptions are just our opinions and these can
be wrong . . . we all make mistakes . . . the more you
forgive others . . . the more you forgive yourself . . .
and the more others forgive you. From now on, you're
never concerned by right and wrong . . . instead
you consider appropriateness . . . you understand
that feelings of love may be wonderful . . . but that
physically displaying these passionate feelings may be
appropriate in some places . . . whilst inappropriate in
others . . . at no point does love ever become bad . . .
romance is part of the loving experience . . . and it too,
can never be bad . . . other people's opinions are just
that . . . opinions . . . these opinions are formed around
the labels . . . that these people have unconsciously
chosen to limit their lives . . . their opinions are their
problems . . . and you don't lose any of your energy
worrying about other people's problems . . . you take
them with a pinch of salt . . . some opinions, however,
are helpful feedback . . . and you'll know in your heart if
they are . . . because you always listen to your heart . . .*

*no matter what may have been said . . . or done . . .
in the past, you are now free . . . no more can an old
hurt affect the way you live your life now . . . you direct
your life . . . no one else . . . you are not a victim . . . you
are free . . . no more could you allow someone to hold
an influence over you . . . because you know that by
your birthright . . . you are equal to anybody on this
planet . . . no one is better than you . . . no one is less
than you . . . no one can take your energy away . . .
only you can give it away . . . you fundamentally
understand . . . that you . . . and only you . . . are
responsible for your wellbeing . . . you make your life
what it is.*

An additional script for enhancing your love life

*Gone are the days spent trying to live your life by other
people's rules . . . gone are the days spent trying to
please everyone else . . . the only person that you set
out to please is yourself . . . you are pleased when you
know . . . that your pleasure did not come at someone
else's expense . . . for you to win, others do not have
to lose . . . you understand the value of living without
sacrifice . . . you are special . . . you're alive . . . you have
been granted the gift of life . . . and that's the whole
gift, including all that comes with it . . . fun, friends,
fulfilment . . . and, of course, love.*

*Sensations change continuously . . . it's a fact of life . . .
some feelings that you once didn't enjoy can become
exquisite . . . anything from looking at a painting . . .
to being complimented . . . can now become truly
beneficial . . . you are always in charge of your body . . .*

and the experience cannot be limited by anyone else's opinions . . . you . . . and only you . . . can be the judge of whether you're enjoying yourself . . . nobody else's judgement counts . . . their labels are worthless in your experience . . . you only concern yourself with what feels good to you . . . and when would be an appropriate time to do something about it . . . maybe straight away, maybe later . . . whichever feels right for you is what's best for you . . . from now on, you instinctively know whether a situation is appropriate . . . in keeping with all things in life.

At all times of your everyday life . . . people can't help but think of you as attractive . . . fun . . . and great company . . . but certainly not somebody who could be pushed around . . . instantly people treat you with more respect . . . because you now treat yourself with more respect . . . people follow your lead . . . no more do you have any time for people who don't respect women . . . or other people's feelings . . . it's your life and you choose who you wish to spend time with.

The men who are attracted to you . . . see you as an equal . . . they see you as someone rather special . . . someone who has self-worth . . . the type of men that you attract . . . now have self-worth . . . like attracts like . . . from now on, all your relationships are based on respect . . . trust . . . and love.

Bliss for those already in a relationship

Without constraints, you are free to enjoy your body to the full . . . relaxed and comfortable with yourself . . . always without trying to please . . . you are now far more aware of the sensations that course through your body . . . far more aware of the sensations flying through your mind . . . so much so that in your love-making . . . all of your awareness . . . is completely absorbed by the exquisite feelings that you're experiencing . . . it's as if each sensation has a note that plays inside you . . . and the different parts of your body play different notes . . . completely relaxed, you gradually become more . . . and more . . . aware of the melody released from within you . . . and the harmony between the two of you . . . now, as you truly let go . . . trusting yourself to the feelings that have guided star-crossed lovers for thousands of years . . . you, too . . . begin to sense the freedom and the music that flood into our lives . . . when we stop thinking and allow our hearts to sing . . . in every moment of your passionate sex . . . all that you sense . . . are your sensational feelings and your rapture . . . quite naturally, your partner feels it too without a word being said . . . as you let go . . . you realize . . . that you're letting go of nothing . . . and in return . . . the reward for your trust . . . is bliss.

Blueprint for Love (men) – for more satisfying relationships

Just allow yourself to relax and become comfortable where you are sitting or lying . . . Think about your feet . . . Notice what your feet are touching . . . now relax those feet and start to think about your breathing . . . Just allow it to become slow and rhythmic . . . and comfortable . . . in fact allow your whole body to relax,

Holding hands is great but, as you know, there's more to life than just holding hands . . . touching is one of the most basic forms of communication . . . and when appropriate, it's also one of the most important forms of communication . . . in fact where emotions are concerned, a genuine hug can say 1,000 words . . . and usually far better than words.

Communicating through words alone is useful in a work environment . . . where consistency and precision may be more important than feelings . . . people, however, are not machines . . . and our most rewarding relationships are those where we can express our feelings . . . in fact, the quality of all our relationships . . . improves as we learn to relate to people, as people.

Because you have chosen to improve your relationships . . . it's one of the best decisions of your life . . . and you recognize the increased happiness created by understanding . . . what makes people feel at ease . . . most people, given the choice, would prefer to be happy rather than sad . . . and to make things easier . . . we tend to choose friends who also like to be happy . . . unpopular people tend to be those who wallow in their problems . . . or derive pleasure from making others unhappy . . . these people often attract illness and bad luck . . . or even other people who feel the same way . . . But you wisely choose to have healthy relationships.

From now on, you always remember that people would prefer to see your best side . . . because your best side is who you really are . . . we always see people at their worst . . . when they get defensive . . . when we get defensive, we're no better . . . gone are the days when you'd invite unhelpful or disruptive people into your life . . . the best way to greet new people is with a friendly attitude and to take each moment as it comes . . . no matter what someone looks like . . . no matter who they may remind you of . . . no matter who they sound like . . . anyone can be your friend . . . knowing this makes your body language more approachable and makes you look more friendly . . . the more friendly you look, the more people will trust you . . . the more you socialize, the easier you find it to recognize people who are trustworthy and considerate . . . you do this by listening carefully to what they say . . . and by observing the way they treat others . . . and by the way they treat you.

The more time you spend with these people . . . the more you recognize your own worth . . . you enjoy spending time with them . . . and they enjoy spending time with you . . . quite naturally, you understand people's likes and dislikes . . . your listening skills continuously improve and bring ever greater rewards . . . you now find that you can introduce people to others that you feel they would be compatible with.

Relationships are the same the whole world over . . . if you are compatible and you trust each other, there is a basis for a relationship . . . after that, everything hinges on the honesty each of you has about your feelings . . . the more honest you are . . . the happier you are . . . you never do things just trying to please someone . . . because by living a lie, you know you only delay the inevitable . . . saying what you feel avoids you bottling up your feelings . . . when you talk about your emotions, you assert yourself naturally . . . you find no need to raise your voice and you explain yourself in a calm but purposeful way . . . this way, your partner recognizes the importance of what you're saying . . . and finds it easy to listen to you . . . in return, you do the same for them and your relationships thrive.

Touching is a natural part of our body language, which communicates directly with our emotions . . . whilst body language is a whole language in itself . . . you already know when someone looks comfortable and when someone does not . . . just as you like your space to be respected . . . you are both aware and respectful of other people's space.

An additional script for those already in a relationship

All relationships are built on trust and all parties must be fully consenting . . . you make sure you always check how comfortable people are around you . . . you do this by observing their body language . . . and by talking to them . . . and then making the appropriate adjustments to the way that you relate to the person that you are with . . . whenever you're in doubt . . . you mention it gently . . . so that you can both talk about your feelings . . . and begin to feel comfortable again.

You enjoy having relaxed and meaningful relationships . . . finding that this is the healthiest environment in which trust can grow . . . intimacy is achieved as both of you progressively drop the barriers that prevent you from being totally honest with each other . . . all your relationships benefit from your new behaviour . . . which also brings a more profound understanding of people and their desires . . . it also allows you to be more honest with your own self.

Quite naturally . . . through healthy communication . . . there will be someone who really relates to you . . . someone whose company you really enjoy . . . comfortable with them, you are now able to explore a greater level of intimacy . . . you know that there's no urgency . . . and that the relationship has its own pace . . . all the time you are able to communicate your feelings . . . and are also in touch with the feelings of your partner . . . our bodies love to be touched . . . that's why we're made the way we are . . . you acknowledge that there are few pleasures in life greater than being intimate with someone you trust and care for.

You enjoy taking your time and understand that there's no correct way to do anything . . . you just listen to your heart and do what feels right . . . it's like a journey . . . you could take the motorway . . . but you choose to take the scenic route . . . you're not just interested in

*getting there . . . you want to savour every moment . . .
really enjoying the journey . . . you allow yourself lots of
time and find out what your partner's likes are . . . your
partner deeply appreciates your tenderness . . . and
the rewards are . . . really touching . . . you sense and
feel love like never before . . . and the sexual expression
of this passion flows through you with ease . . . you
experiment, take breaks . . . and find it easy to keep
your sense of fun . . . loving has never been easier . . .
rich in love, you blossom . . . and every day your life just
gets better . . . and better.*

Scripts for recovering from a broken relationship

Recovering from a broken relationship can also be one of
those situations where there is no 'resolution' or closure,
as inevitably we ask the question 'why?' but invariably
never get an answer. The mind gets full and overloaded,
leading to more stress and upset, and self-hypnosis can be
an excellent solution. The Progressive Relaxation induction
(*see page 51*) will undoubtedly help with relaxation and
the words in your selected suggestion will have a powerful
effect on the inner mind.

The conscious 'thinking about' the situation almost never
resolves the feelings of loss but using or adapting one
of the following self-hypnosis scripts may help to heal
things at a deeper level. It's often a domino effect where
drawing a line under a past relationship opens you up to
new possibilities, and the sooner you use self-hypnosis the
faster you can help to heal yourself.

When you have loved and lost

Every trauma, problem and obstacle that has happened in the past has been put to use . . . in building up your strength and your character . . . to allow you to begin to see your future more clearly . . . more positively than ever before . . . your emotions now begin to settle down . . . the anger, the frustration and the hurt you felt before . . . which got in the way of your decision-making . . . are now back in their correct places . . . leaving valuable information . . . from experience . . . that will enable you to draw better and more constructive conclusions . . . the emotions settle down . . . no longer on the surface . . . no longer in the way of your thinking clearly . . . they have served their purpose and because your mind is now stronger . . . clearer . . . and more positive than before . . . you begin to feel the benefits . . . your confidence is stronger and healthier . . . you believe in yourself . . . as a person . . . and a woman/man . . . you enjoy your new respect and no longer carry hurt around with you . . . like a damp bundle of dirty washing . . . instead you are proud of yourself and your new attitude . . . your attitude is no longer a problem.

You realize that if people say hurtful things it is because they have a problem . . . and are frustrated . . . you can understand that the remarks and the actions . . . that would have hurt you in the past may be a retaliation . . . retaliation for a hurt they were experiencing . . . it does not prevent you from examining yourself to check whether it is your fault . . .

*but this time you are able to do so in a constructive
way . . . and you are able to work on your faults and
weaknesses to enable you to grow and . . . be happy . . .
and contented.*

*Your subconscious inner mind works at overcoming
your weaknesses . . . the weaknesses that have
caused you so much mental anguish . . . resulting in a
wonderful peace of mind . . . as your emotions settle . . .
new, positive emotions now come to the surface . . .
replacing the old, useless, negative emotions . . .
happiness . . . a sense of humour and a love of life
replace . . . anxiety . . . hurt . . . and anger.*

*The bad habit of worrying is minimized . . . it is
unproductive and destructive . . . because now your
mind is open to positive thoughts and you find that
you visualize yourself easily and often as happy . . .
smiling . . . ready to enjoy the wonderful experiences
your life has to offer . . . this very action indicates to
your subconscious . . . your inner mind . . . what you
wish . . . and your subconscious will be instructed by
the language of visualization to follow your wishes . . .
resulting in your happiness.*

The end of a relationship

*You are a confident . . . self-assured . . . independent
person . . . fully able to satisfy your own requirements
yourself without being dependent on or affected
by another person . . . your self-love is more than
adequate . . . it lets you be perfectly at home with*

yourself . . . you are fully aware of your own sexuality and recognize your abundant ability to love and be loved . . . you have cleared all of your past incompatibilities . . . and are totally at home with the past . . . knowing that it has no hold over you any more . . . you are extremely happy when you see your previous partner is following their own dreams . . . when you see them . . . they will remind you how much freedom and independence you now hold . . . now you can focus all your energies into fulfilling your ambitions and dreams . . . allowing space for someone who can give you all that you could wish for and more.

You feel stronger . . . healthier . . . more vibrant and full of self-love . . . your energy is increased as you open up to all the possibilities available to you . . . this new-found source of energy and your greater sense of awareness allow you to feel more . . . see . . . more . . . enjoy all that you experience as if for the first time . . . your confidence is so strong . . . you are at home with yourself . . . whether alone in bed at night . . . or out meeting new people . . . when you prepare for sleep . . . you look forward to luxuriating in the expanse of your own bed . . . feeling exhilarated at being able to do anything you want . . . without answering to any other.

Your self-assurance completely obliterates all those tiny fears that may have plagued you in the past . . . you feel secure and safe, knowing that your environment is strongly protected by its powerful energy.

. . . .

Deep-rooted issues that can affect relationships

As illustrated in the case history where a cat phobia had been caused by a fear of thunder (*see page 17*), sometimes we don't know where our behaviour comes from, as the answers are locked away in our subconscious mind. The same is true for relationships – our past is often reflected in our present behaviour. People often identify repeating patterns in relationships, but have no idea where they came from or, more importantly, how to stop them. Some well-formed self-hypnosis suggestions can eradicate many problems but sometimes you need a qualified hypnotherapist to help identify and resolve more deep-seated issues.

Katie Glen, a psychologist and outstanding therapist, has shared two case histories, which perfectly illustrate how sophisticated the mind can be. These cases required age regression, where a professional, skilled hypnotherapist takes the client back to a point where a trauma or life-changing incident occurred, often when they were a young child. In both cases, the clients were able to move forward with their life whereas without hypnotherapy they would probably still be stuck in the same situation.

Case study

Natalie was distressed about her latest love-life disaster. She was in a messy relationship with a man who had duped her into thinking he was single. Not long into the relationship, Natalie discovered he was in a long-term relationship with a live-in partner, whom he had no real intention of leaving.

This was just one of several disastrous liaisons in which Natalie had played second fiddle to her lover's life. Previously, she had had a torrid affair with a married man at work, which resulted in her leaving her job. She had also had an on-off relationship with someone else for over seven years, who would never take her out or show her off. Eventually he ran off and married someone else within months.

During regression therapy, a pattern of behaviour, which stemmed from her childhood, was found. Her subconscious had taken it on board that she was second best and not worth standing up for. Once this information was brought forward to her conscious mind, Natalie quickly forgot about the previous lover and, within a couple of weeks, had met a wonderful man. Five years later, Natalie is happily married with a lovely baby son.

Case study

Paul wanted help... FAST! As a married man with two young children he was devastated to discover his wife, whom he'd been in a relationship with for over nine years, was having an affair.

The situation was affecting every part of his life, including his relationship with his children, his career and his health. In an intensive hypnotherapy session, Paul identified the problem. He found he had experienced other, not dissimilar dysfunctional relationships prior to meeting his wife, and had a pattern of being attracted to very controlling women. Some powerful suggestions helped relieve the stress, pain and anger he was experiencing, allowing him to rationalize the situation and create a solution for moving forward, thereby supporting both his children's and his needs.

In his own words, Paul explained: 'Less stressed and our divorce will be as easy, quick and painless as possible. Going into my first session and being asked what I wanted out of my life and relationships helped me focus on what I wanted for the first time. I was able to accept that my relationship has broken down, I am now much clearer about how to move forward, and feel I can now identify what is important to me rather than repeating the same old nightmare relationship patterns. I am also determined to find a satisfactory solution that will work for my children, my soon-to-be-ex-wife and myself.'

I have only included a selection of scripts for relationships in this chapter, but you can find more help on my website (www.selfhypnosisthebook.com) and information about my relationship package at the back of this book (*see page 190*).

Some relationship problems can be very general but everyone's relationship or situation is different. Try your chosen script at least once just to see how it benefits you before customizing it to your own circumstances. Then if you wish you can add what you believe you need. When you are more experienced, this is the time to make amendments. Don't make the mistake of thinking you do not need some of the suggestions included in the script, as maybe you do without realizing it. Your mind will edit out what it doesn't need.

Self-hypnosis can make life so much easier in relationships by training your mind to clear irrational jealousy, fears of being let down, lack of confidence in relationships and a host of other problems that you can change.

RECAP ✍️

❖ Self-hypnosis can be an enormous benefit for couples, even those who on the surface appear not to have any problems. You can always make improvements however good your relationship seems. Even if you have a wonderful relationship, try to avoid becoming complacent which can create boredom.

❖ You can establish your own 'blueprint' for what you want from your ideal relationship and use self-hypnosis to help manifest your dream partner.

❖ As an alternative to traditional couple's therapy, self-hypnosis is a powerful tool to get relationships back on track and is more often a quicker solution.

❖ You can use the simple suggestions for dealing with a variety of relationships issues or you can personalize them to your own circumstances.

❖ Use the 'Blueprint for Love' suggestions to help you focus on finding your ideal partner. You may also find it is a useful 'top up' to use periodically in order to maintain a healthy relationship.

Chapter 9
Further scripts for self-hypnosis

*'Insanity: doing the same thing over and over
again and expecting different results.'*
ALBERT EINSTEIN

For the past 100 years hypnotherapists have guarded their suggestion scripts like prized possessions, refusing to sell them even to other hypnotherapists because they were so valuable and it would have created competition. Carefully worded suggestions with just the right terminology ensured success and these well-formed suggestions were like gold to the hypnotherapists who found them. They felt it was the difference between the hypnotherapy being successful or not.

Thirty years ago, when I started in practice, there were considerably fewer hypnotherapists than there are today. It was difficult to get hold of *good* scripts, even in hypnosis training books, while they were virtually non-existent in academic books. Until the advent of self-publishing, there were few non-academic books published on the subject of hypnosis and fewer still that included scripts. Doctors and psychologists have always wanted to avoid teaching the public to hypnotize, which led to an air of secrecy around the whole subject of hypnosis.

Trainers on hypnosis courses would sell each script for a handsome amount and the hypnotherapist would then keep it to himself or herself, like a chef not sharing a secret personal recipe. As my practice grew, I realized I needed more scripts for various client issues than those I had bought catered for, so I started creating my own, and had amazing results with them. I shared them with people I trained as part of my hypnotherapy course and they had similar success.

When I wrote my hypnotherapy books I made sure I added plenty of scripts that would be useful, not only to readers, but to hypnotherapists whom I also wanted to read my books. My first book, *Self Hypnosis*, was called their 'Little Gem' by the publisher's managing editor. It consistently sold well month on month and was reprinted many times. Not only was it published internationally and translated into five languages but it was also chosen as recommended reading by many of the training courses in the UK, ensuring regular sales year after year.

Now all my books have been adapted into apps and are sold all over the world, but the point I am making is how important good suggestions are, and what makes the scripts in this book so valuable is that they have been tested over and over again in group therapy and in teaching self-hypnosis, which means they have all been thoroughly tested professionally with clients and so you can be assured of great results.

Nowadays the Internet is a huge resource for scripts. You only have to Google 'hypnosis scripts' and you will be faced with a multitude of pages offering them for sale and even a selection for free. But by learning the rules on how to construct a script in Chapter 6, you will be able to choose the workable scripts with confidence. What you can be sure of is that the scripts included here haven't just been made up to sound good, but are carefully worded for maximum impact.

The scripts in this chapter are designed to get the very best out of your self-hypnosis – to help you overcome all sorts of negative thoughts and behaviours by improving any aspects of your life you want to change.

The general rules for creating suggestions are covered in Chapter 6, and the rules say not to use too many negative words. This should be monitored with common sense, as there is a mistaken belief that the inner mind won't accept negative words and disregards the word 'not' or 'don't'. For example, if you were trying to program the idea 'I never overeat' or 'I will not smoke', the theory is that the mind eliminates the negative word 'not' or 'don't', leaving you with the instruction 'I overeat' or 'I smoke'. However, in my experience this is not the case. For years I have had negative words in my 'Stop smoking' script (*see page 165*) and I've been able to show a 95 per cent success rate. Another example is the stage hypnotist who tells their volunteer that they can't get out of their chair or unlock their hands and, as hard as they try, they find they can't, due to the inner mind literally accepting the negative suggestion. The result is that they are unable to unclasp their hands until the hypnotist tells them to. Therefore you may find that there are a few negative words in some of the scripts; however, their use is limited and they are strong, effective and proven to work.

As mentioned earlier, your success rate for using these self-help methods depends considerably on your commitment, the script you use, the seriousness with which it is executed and whether a problem is trauma-related or not.

Constantly checking phones and social media

As mentioned in Chapter 7 (*see page 107*), people nowadays spend a lot of time using their mobile devices, which can interfere with social occasions and quality time with partners, friends and family. Use this script if you want to reduce the time spent using your mobile phone or tablet and claim back that valuable time.

Because you want to have a life . . . some freedom to enjoy your time . . . you have decided to choose certain times to be switched off from the Internet . . . you find it is so easy to retrain yourself to stop constantly checking your messages, news and social media. Now you have freedom . . . lots of freedom . . . in fact as much as you choose. What a relief that everything is properly done! . . . You have finished all your work online . . . you are so relieved now . . . nothing bothers you any more . . . you have no more need to worry . . . you have finished writing your emails and checking your social networks and it is now time to switch off . . . literally switch off all your gadgets . . . the gadgets mean . . . you computer, your smartphone, your tablet, etc. . . . . whatever you use for checking . . . You have chosen a time that suits you to switch off . . . You can leave your landline on if you wish but all other phones can be silenced or switched off completely . . . No more temptation to look and check . . . this is your special time to get a life . . . Your time to live and become free of the habit you have learned . . . The good news is that because you learned this very bad habit of constantly checking . . . you can learn not to do it any more . . . your subconscious now helps you and reprograms your inner mind to know what is important and what isn't . . . you learn to trust your subconscious. The result will be plenty of spare time to enjoy your reading, sports, TV, radio, or hobbies. You now have a life.

You know your friends will be looking forward to hearing from you . . . knowing that you have taken the trouble to keep in touch . . . but not overdoing it.

. . . .

Hyp-notes

The German government has become worried about their workers' mental health. So much so that they are now considering making it illegal to email colleagues after 6 p.m. They found there to be a strong connection between constant availability online and the increase in mental illness.

Becoming people friendly

Because you no longer fear the unknown . . . the benefits to your social . . . domestic . . . and work life are limitless . . . You are happier each day because you enjoy meeting people and being in their company . . . and you enjoy and look forward to being in new places or situations . . . new places excite you.

With this new-found freedom you find that your personality is able to develop . . . exactly how you want it to be . . . you may want to be dynamic . . . you may want to be a good listener . . . you may want to be more up front . . . whatever you choose you find you attract and enjoy the company of the type of people you wish . . . who give you the friendship and companionship you are seeking.

You are happy in the knowledge that you have a more contented . . . exciting and dynamic lifestyle . . . as you find it more and more easy to go out and socialize with friends of both sexes.

The world is a happy, friendly and safe place to enjoy . . . a place to meet people and to achieve fulfilment . . . a place to enjoy a new-found confidence in yourself.

As you enjoy the company of your friends . . . they also enjoy your spontaneous and confident humour . . . you are realizing your full potential.

Fear of ageing

It is because you wish to be happy . . . accepting yourself . . . that you want to age gracefully . . . ageing gracefully . . . is an art form . . . and has little or nothing . . . to do with looks . . .

All your life you have known . . . that you can't judge a book by its cover . . . and you have found . . . that there are far more meaningful criteria . . . than looks . . . that make up a person's worth.

We live in a society . . . obsessed by sell-by dates . . . You have become aware of this . . . and those obsessed with beauty and youth spend absurd amounts of money . . . trying to be something . . . that they are not . . . You have really begun to appreciate . . . that a person who is healthy and happy . . . is richer than any fool . . . who comforts themself . . . displaying the status symbols and money . . .

You can now see that this state of affairs . . . is made by the most deluded . . . paying others to bolster their vanity . . . unfortunately this quest . . . for the elixir of youth . . . prevents our society from ageing gracefully . . .

Sooner or later they will learn . . . putting their money to better use . . . but in the meantime . . . you honour your body's needs . . . You eat a varied . . . healthy and exciting diet . . . and you maintain a lifestyle . . . that allows you to exercise regularly . . . and enjoy the company of good friends . . . You sleep well at night . . . and you pick your friends carefully . . . As you know . . . Your worth is in your experience . . . in what you have learned . . . and what you can share . . . It's how you are . . . not what you pretend to be . . . and you know that every line on your face . . . has earned its place . . .

They say a face without lines . . . is the face of the fool . . . a facelift can't change . . . the person inside . . . and poor is the man . . . whose skin is his pride . . .

Panic attacks

This is a very good time to take stock . . . a time to truly seize the opportunity to help yourself . . . a time to be thankful for just how good life has been . . . For in those times when we think we've given up hope . . . things still work out fine for us . . . at the time we feel crushed by self-doubt . . . all that . . . is now in the past.

It is now in the past . . . because that is how it was meant to be . . . For our highest possible learning . . . times of doubt . . . present to us the best possible way to learn the value . . . of making calm decisions . . . Now you understand that time is on your side . . . not against you . . . and you have learned that by speaking up early you can prevent problems later on . . . from a place of calm . . .

You don't speak up because you have something to prove . . . you speak up because what you have to say is important . . . it is important because you have considered your message and you do not wish to devalue the importance of your words . . .

You have finally learned to assert yourself . . . because you know that your opinion is as valid as anyone else's. You have now learned that the people are convinced by your honest, logical and calm manner and words . . . They are more than happy to discuss your views . . . The panic that you have felt in the past has acted as your teacher . . . it has taught you to observe . . . and more importantly, it has shown you . . . how easy it is . . . to be one of the sheep . . .

No more . . . No more and never again will you be a sheep . . . You once felt panic because you felt powerless . . . now you know that because you are now taking more time to notice everything . . . taking time in a calm and even playful way . . . that you are able to express your feelings quite clearly . . . Every day you are able to use fewer words to say what you want . . . every day you are becoming more eloquent . . . and as a reward this makes you appear . . . even more attractive.

The greatest gift anyone can learn from panic . . . is clarity . . . this gift is yours now . . . and it rings out like the shepherd's bell . . .

Dentist anxiety

Picture yourself now . . . so very relaxed . . . you have practised relaxation so that you find it is easy to slip into a relaxed state . . . and to your surprise, when you think of the dentist you no longer feel anything but calm . . . knowing that you can just calm yourself whenever you feel the need to do so . . .

You travel to the dentist you begin to feel the luxury of calm . . . floating over you . . . as you enter the surgery . . . you do not mind waiting . . . you can easily use the time reading or daydreaming of pleasant memories . . . this is your special time . . . When you are called into the surgery to have the work done you feel very calm and relaxed . . . the sight of the instruments or room just serve to allow you to be calm and comfortable . . . knowing you are looking after your teeth . . . As the dentist starts to work on your teeth you relax even more . . . any work that the dentist does . . . brings no discomfort at all . . . you just notice the work and the sounds with idle curiosity . . . you allow yourself to relax even more and daydream about wonderful memories or wishes you would like to bestow on yourself . . . If the dentist talks to you . . . you respond easily and effortlessly . . . He or she may be surprised by your calmness . . . and may even say so . . . you just find the whole procedure easy and relaxing, knowing that the work is necessary and that you will be happy with the results.

Fear of flying

You find that you can relax now whenever you would like to . . . when you are in a situation that before might have caused you anxiety when there was no need for it . . . you take a deep breath and a wave of relaxation flows through your body . . . As you feel so calm and relaxed, you imagine you are setting off for the airport . . . you are surprised and happy to realize that you feel relaxed and comfortable about the journey . . . you imagine the trip to the airport . . . you arrive at the airport and check your baggage in and you feel so calm and relaxed . . . ready for the flight and looking forward to arriving at your destination . . . it is now time to go to the departure lounge . . . as you walk along, you casually look out of the windows and see the planes taking off and landing . . . some are parked ready to take on more passengers . . . you find the sight relaxing and as you take a deep breath, you find yourself even more calm and relaxed.

The time goes very quickly as you await your boarding call . . . when it is announced you are looking forward to getting onto the plane and making yourself comfortable for the flight . . . you feel very comfortable and relaxed as you walk along the corridor to board the plane . . . you board the plane and find your seat . . . you feel very calm and relaxed as you watch the flight attendant giving you your instructions . . . the plane starts to taxi to the runway and you look out of the window and, as you do, a wonderful feeling of calm flows through you . . . as the plane revs its engines ready for take-off, you feel confident . . . the engine noises relax you even more . . . as the plane takes off and settles into flight, you feel a wave of relaxation flow through you . . . and you realize you feel content and comfortable . . . you may decide to doze or read, have a conversation or even watch the in-flight film . . . whatever your choice is, you find you are enjoying the flight and you take advantage of the comforts offered.

The plane now begins to make its descent ready to land and, as you take a deep breath, you relax and enjoy the descent of the plane . . . the plane lands and as you prepare to disembark, you feel refreshed and enthusiastic . . . you look back on the flight and realize you have enjoyed the journey.

Weight control

Because you want to lose weight and become healthier and fitter . . . each day you eat the food that you know is good for you . . . You enjoy healthy food . . . You no longer crave high-calorie rich foods and enjoy eating low-calorie healthy foods . . . Your subconscious knows which foods are good for you and allows you to lose weight at the rate suitable for your body . . . Day by day you eat only when you are physically hungry . . . and you eat and want only those foods that are good for your body . . . You always sit down when you eat and enjoy drinking water . . . You find it very cool and refreshing and you like the taste . . . Your stomach is smaller . . . and getting smaller with every day that passes . . . You visualize your stomach as small.

The moment you recognize you want to live a full life as a healthy person . . . your life changes . . . you broaden your horizons and enhance the quality of your life . . . second best, no more . . . you can wear nice clothes . . .

enjoy a better lifestyle . . . have self-confidence . . . and no limits . . . that's what's in store for you.

A suitable change emerges . . . you are happy to trade rich food . . . for a richer life . . . making a decision and sticking to it not only enhances your life, it also raises your self-esteem . . . you'll be amazed at just how many things in your life will change so effortlessly . . . the thought of exercise actually becomes appealing and it's as if you are getting younger . . . You always leave food on your plate . . . and day by day you are enjoying a new eating habit . . . You only think of the bite that is in your mouth . . . and because you think only of the bite that is in your mouth, you enjoy the taste of it much more . . . Your taste buds become more sensitive . . . and you get much more satisfaction from each bite . . . You eat more slowly . . . you eat much less . . . but you enjoy it more . . . You are looking better and you are feeling better . . . You feel good about yourself.

Sugar addiction

Comfort eating is like an addictive drug . . . you are on a short 'high' when you satisfy your cravings, but it then leads to a vicious circle . . . sugar gives you this quick high . . . but too much is so very bad for you . . . it is addictive . . . it is in so many savoury foods now . . . you have decided to check the labels for sugar in your food . . . you can get hooked so very easily . . . That is why type 2 diabetes is now an epidemic and due to too much sugar . . . many sparkling drinks can have as much as nine teaspoons of sugar in them . . . The sugar in real and organic fruit is not the same . . . it is digested properly and naturally . . . it is the processed sugar and too much of it that is your enemy . . . you have now decided to look after your body and cut out so much of the sugar you have been eating . . . it is easy . . . you find you no longer want too much sugar . . .

Alcohol (for the drinker who wants to change)

This script is suitable if you want to give up alcohol altogether. When I worked in Malaysia there were a lot of expats who drank very heavily, and it was affecting their work and even their social life. I gained a reputation for helping these heavy drinkers quit. I was able to check with my clients after 10 years and they were still not drinking. One client, who became rather unpleasant when he drank, even bought a bar. He didn't even have the urge to drink but just enjoyed his life more and was very sociable, which delighted his friends.

I want you to picture yourself throwing all the alcohol away . . . see yourself pouring the alcohol down the drain . . . accept that you are killing yourself with alcohol . . . and you want your body to look after you . . . and you want your body to be fit and healthy – not disturbed by manmade chemicals, that only serve to disrupt your mind's balance and your body's working.

To you alcohol is a poison . . . all alcohol can give you is a shorter life and poor health . . . and getting old before you need to . . . Alcohol is a depressant . . . it can't give you anything because it is a depressant. Why do you think some people cry when they are drunk – because it is a depressant. You will accept yourself as a teetotaller . . . You don't want to drink any more. You can get high with your friends without alcohol; you can get high on the atmosphere and ambience. You find you enjoy drinking water . . . it feels cleansing and healthy.

Accepting that you don't need it any more . . . you feel wonderful and when someone offers you an alcoholic drink . . . you say 'no thanks' and you feel exhilarated.

You are now and forever a confirmed teetotaller. Your final decision is made and agreed to, and every day that passes reinforces it.

Picture in your mind someone offering you a drink. You always answer, 'No.' You say that proudly. Every time you refuse an offer of a drink, you feel an invigorating sense of power and pride. You are proud of being one of those envied people that have the ability and the drive to see drink as the depressant it is . . . and do not want it. You have the guts and the motivation to not want it.

You always enjoy the pleasant, relaxed feeling of self-hypnosis, and you have an overwhelming desire to go into self-hypnosis every day. You always feel completely rejuvenated and refreshed when you come out of hypnosis, because the complete, restful relaxation causes your body to become completely normalized.

Your blood pressure is normal . . . your glands are working in harmony with one another . . . your body chemistry is balanced . . . and you feel good.

Now just relax even more and enjoy a moment of silence . . . during which all of these true ideas and concepts make a deep and lasting impression upon your subconscious mind . . . never to be removed. This moment of silence starts now . . .

Anxiety

It is because you now wish to savour life to the full . . . taking advantage of all the opportunities that come your way . . . that you have now chosen to reclaim your life . . . allowing an old habit to drop . . . into permanent retirement.

There have been times . . . when things just seemed to get out of hand . . . times when you didn't feel in control . . . and a bit of anxiety crept in . . . it happens to everyone . . . it's a very important lesson that we all have to learn . . . Sooner or later we all have to learn about focusing our energy . . . in our everyday lives we have tasks to overcome . . . some have obvious solutions . . . whilst others will require us to learn and grow . . . The greatest cause of anxiety is a lack of familiarity . . . over time, all things become familiar . . . over time we become proficient . . . as if we've done these things all our lives . . .

*We distress ourselves by worrying that we or someone
we care for . . . is not yet ready for certain tasks . . .
We needn't worry because in this life . . . we tend
to learn as we go along . . . and the proof is in the
results . . . You are now in that wonderful place of
self-acceptance . . . ready to go forward . . . living
without anxiety . . . Deep down you already know that
worrying is a waste of your valuable energy . . . You
are becoming more and more aware that when you
move your energy towards a solution . . . your energy
either makes things simpler . . . or more complicated . . .
worrying always complicate things.*

*In the future you will instantly become aware of
when you are anxious . . . and you will find yourself
remembering it is never worth worrying . . . and that
every time this happens your life will change . . .
because important events are about to take place.*

*You are now aware that in every situation where you
must choose between two options . . . that there is
always a third option . . . which is to do nothing . . .
Often things sort themselves out fine . . . without us
having to tinker with them . . .*

*You have also learned not to presume that there is a
problem . . . where none exists. Virtually all the world's
greatest discoveries have resulted from accidents
or unexpected outcomes . . . Learning to appreciate
the gift of the unfamiliar is the very quality shared by
those . . . most considered to be geniuses . . . Now
that you can recognize the feeling of the unfamiliar
approaching . . . you are better placed than most . . .*

to keep your eyes open for the potential opportunities about to blossom . . . What was once your biggest worry . . . is now a major key to your happiness and success . . . and life just gets better and better . . .

Sleep (insomnia)

Imagine in your mind's eye . . . that you are reclining in a comfortable garden . . . on a very comfortable garden bench . . . The temperature is just right . . . for you . . . And you feel so comfortable . . . You have decided to go to sleep . . . and are now going to help your inner mind . . . get into a new habit . . . of easy . . . comfortable . . . safe . . . sleep. After a very short time . . . you will find you do not need . . . to practise . . . you will just lie down . . . and close your eyes . . . and drift into a beautiful sleep . . . but this exercise is to retrain you . . . to sleep quickly . . . and easily.

You use an awful lot of energy staying awake . . . now if you sleep and rest yourself thoroughly . . . you have an oversupply of energy when you awaken.

So let us begin . . . I want you to imagine . . . that just in front of you . . . are some steps . . . that lead to a lower part . . . of the garden. You notice there are about ten steps . . . and a few feet away . . . at the bottom of the steps . . . you will notice . . . a large . . . oak . . . door . . . that is surrounded . . . by a very large stone wall . . . You cannot see behind the door . . . but instinctively you know that it is a special . . . place . . . for you . . . you may prefer . . . to be by the side . . . of a lake . . . a soft running stream . . . or even by the ocean . . . or you may prefer the countryside . . . whatever you choose . . . you just know . . . that the special place behind the door . . . is exactly what you want . . . now I want you to go over to the steps . . . and instinctively knowing that . . . with every step . . . you will go deeper . . . and deeper . . . into deep . . . calm . . . relaxation, . . . even deeper . . . than you are right now . . . and each night you hear these . . . suggestions you find . . . it is easier . . . and quicker . . . to relax . . . and you may find you go to sleep . . . before the end of these suggestions . . . and you may even find that just lying down to listen to the tape allows you to go sound asleep. So let's begin . . . In your mind's eye . . . put your foot on the first step . . . and feel yourself going into a deeper . . . and deeper . . . and deeper . . . into relaxation . . . Now putting your foot on the second step . . . feel yourself going even deeper . . . and deeper . . . now . . . onto the third step . . . going deeper . . . and deeper and deeper . . . relaxed. Each step doubles . . . your relaxation.

Down onto the fourth step . . . going deeper and deeper . . . now putting your foot onto the fifth step . . . going even deeper still . . . Stepping onto the next step . . . takes you even deeper . . . onto the next step . . . going deeper still . . . onto the eighth step . . . deeper still . . . down onto the next step . . . and as you reach the bottom step . . . you notice a big oak door . . . You walk over to the door . . . and as you gently push it open . . . you feel a feeling of peace . . . and relaxation . . . as you notice how beautiful . . . your special place is. You imagine yourself lying down peacefully asleep your breath rhythmic and comfortable and you sleep soundly . . .

Now notice the colour . . . of the flowers . . . the drifting clouds . . . the birds singing, the rustling of the leaves . . . the pleasant warmth of the sun . . . continue to visualize your special place . . . picture yourself comfortably . . . lying down . . . watching the leaves . . . as they fall from the trees nearby . . . reminding you that it is possible to let go of all your problems . . . and worries . . . allowing them to drop away . . . just like old leaves dropping away from trees making way for new growth. And as you concentrate on your breathing, you drift comfortably into deep relaxation and sleep.

You now look forward to going to bed . . . you look forward to climbing into your bed . . . Visualize your alarm clock it may be one you have where you sleep or it may be one that you create in your inner mind . . . bring it forward in your inner mind so you can see it clearly . . . Now stick the hands on the clock at the time you want to wake up.

Fix your eyes on that spot and focus them on that spot for a few moments . . . instructing your subconscious mind. Your subconscious will select the special depth of sleep to ensure you awaken totally refreshed . . .

You look forward to experiencing that beautiful restful sleep which enables your body and mind to work in a beautiful balanced harmonious way.

Stress relief

Stress can creep in at any time and can be due to a large number of factors from work to personal issues, such as relationships or money worries and the pace of modern life leaving you feeling overwhelmed. However, whatever the reason, suggestions in self-hypnosis can improve your enthusiasm to succeed and give you the confidence to do so. Before using the following script, try the Orange Liquid suggestion (*see page 57*), to detox your mind then you may want to consider adding something that is personal to you.

I want you to picture yourself emptying your mind of all the unpleasant . . . memories . . . and feelings . . . and worries you have . . . I want you to discard them . . . throw them into a container . . . seal it up . . . and have it taken away . . . Now you have a chance to start anew with your life . . . with control . . . no unpleasant thoughts that corrupt your thinking . . . You now have control of your life and you have choices . . . Experience how it feels . . . how good it feels . . . Any new problems that arise . . . you find easy to deal with. Instead of problems you think of them as challenges and let you inner mind find solutions that are easy and comfortable. You don't even have to work at it . . . Your inner mind does it for you while you are getting on with your life.

Picture yourself emptying your mind of all the unpleasant thoughts, memories and feelings you have collected through the years . . . you can do this by imagining you are using a gigantic suction vacuum cleaner . . . sucking all the negative thoughts out of your mind . . . there is now plenty of space to fill up with wonderful thoughts . . . This is easy . . . all you do is instruct your subconscious to do a search in your mind for all the positive and constructive thoughts that will be useful to you . . . The mind is so sophisticated it can do this in a split second . . . Now use your imagination and pretend that you only have nice thoughts . . . let your imagination start to roll. Imagine your life . . . your future with just a positive outlook. Picture yourself with this positive attitude . . . and now look at what your imagination has come up with . . . explore this wonderful area . . . Your inner mind will be able to show you the way forward . . . take a moment to let your imagination picture your future filled with positivity and pleasure . . .

[Pause for about a minute.]

Whenever you wish to look at your life more clearly you can use this technique to allow your mind to advise you . . . Remember your inner mind has all the answers to your problems. It has the information to give you the best advice . . . take advantage of this facility . . . take some time out of your day to build your plan . . . Your inner mind will be there at any time to help you.

Hyp-notes

Coincidence? When I wrote my first book *Self Hypnosis* in 1992 my stop smoking therapy was so successful that I went round the world training the technique. Whilst working for a few years in Malaysia I became so famous for helping people quit smoking that the Health

Minister publicly endorsed my stop smoking therapy. That was over 20 years ago and now one of my talented students is a leading teacher of hypnosis specializing in stopping smoking. With his dedication and a lot of hard work, he too has just earned an award as recognition for stop smoking therapy, also presented by the current Minister of Health of Malaysia.

Stop smoking

This main script has been used, unaltered, for years and forms a part of my 'Stop Smoking In One Hour' technique.

You have now made one of the most important decisions of your life . . . to save your life . . . by giving up smoking . . . giving up polluting your lungs . . . your lungs perform one of the most important functions in your body . . . without them you cannot breathe . . . you cannot live . . . it is essential for you to keep your lungs clean and fill them with fresh air . . . so you can live . . . and be healthy.

Your body has to cope with pollution from the air that you breathe . . . your lungs are adaptable and can cope with this . . . but the extra strain that smoking brings about . . . the extra concentrated pollution you are sucking in from each cigarette . . . is weakening your insides . . . your mouth . . . your throat . . . your lungs . . . your stomach, and your blood . . . are just a few of the victims of your carelessness . . . but also the dangerous chemicals that are used in the pesticides sprayed on the tobacco as it grows are used to kill insects . . . and now are slowly but surely killing you . . . you have been forcing people around you . . . even young children . . . to breathe in your extra pollution . . . you have been ignorant of how unsociable it has become . . . no more . . . now you care about yourself and the people around you.

From now on . . . you will find that you are more and more conscious . . . that smoking is bad for you . . . you are more and more aware . . . of the damage it is doing to your health . . . that it is increasing . . . by many times your chances of dying . . . a horrible and painful death . . . from cancer or heart disease . . . you imagine yourself fighting and struggling for breath . . . or suffering with severe damage to your limbs and arteries.

You may fool yourself . . . that this . . . is a long way off . . . but you know it may . . . catch up with you eventually . . . if you carry on smoking . . . you know that smoking is doing serious damage . . . to your limbs and arteries.

You may fool yourself . . . that this . . . is a long way off . . . but you know it will catch up with you eventually . . . you know that smoking is doing serious damage to your general level of fitness . . . you hate the unpleasant taste in your mouth and throat . . . you hate the way that smoke makes your hair and clothes smell . . . especially when you know that other people around you . . . are noticing it, too . . . so many people have been able to give up now . . . and they notice it more when you smell of smoke . . . even being beside you makes their own clothes smell.

You know how much smoking is costing you and how much better you can spend the money on other things . . . you know that deep down you are lying to yourself . . . when you tell yourself that smoking calms and relaxes you . . . it's only a crutch – you can cope easily without it . . . you know it is really only making you more tense . . . it is no longer sociable, in fact the smoker is now a misfit . . . a danger to non-smokers . . . forcing them to become passive smokers . . . against their will.

You find the thought of a cigarette . . . so disgusting . . . that you do not want to even pick one up . . . from now on you cut off any urge to have a cigarette . . . before it even strikes you . . . by relaxing . . . and slowing down your breathing . . . as you do this the urge to smoke . . . disappears . . . your subconscious is finding ways to get rid of your smoking habit . . . redirecting the satisfaction . . . to a good habit . . . more advantageous to you . . . you have no desire at all from now on to smoke . . . your craving has gone . . . forever.

The whole idea of smoking is offensive to you . . . you just don't need it any more . . . your inner mind finds safe and effective ways to rid yourself of this . . . revolting habit . . . and as your complete mastery . . . over your former smoking habit increases . . . you become proud of your self-control and willpower . . . your lungs and throat . . . feel so much clearer . . . you have much more energy . . . you feel so much more relaxed . . . even food tastes so much better . . . and you enjoy it so much more . . . although you find

*your appetite doesn't increase . . . you feel more like
eating healthy foods . . . and so you find you are able
to maintain your desired weight much more easily . . .
while protecting your body . . . from the poison of
further smoking . . . your inner mind automatically
balancing your food intake . . . to keep you fit and
healthy . . . your resistance to illness and disease
increases steadily day by day . . . now just take a deep
breath . . . and relax . . . now take a deep breath . . .
and relax.*

Scripts for phobias

Anxiety can create panic attacks, and panic attacks can
be linked to an unspecified phobia. Panic attacks, phobias
and anxiety go hand in hand. Fear of cars, driving, sex,
motorways, bridges, tubes, planes, spiders, snakes and
new phobias are rife now because of our busy world full
of technology and change. Hypnosis has always been the
most successful of all the therapies so this can be your
chance to get rid of that irritating phobia.

Agoraphobia

*Relax your body . . . let your body go limp . . . and
comfortable . . . allow yourself the luxury of releasing
all the tension . . . help yourself along by slowly . . .
and lavishly . . . taking in a deep breath . . . now gently
and slowly let that breath out . . . emptying your lungs
completely . . . breathe in slowly once again and now
let that breath out calmly and comfortably . . . Once*

again, breathe in slowly and notice how you feel so
much more relaxed . . . and you now begin to release
that breath . . . see your body loosening . . . floating
through what is happening . . . that wonderful . . .
pure . . . relaxation . . . allowing time to pass . . .
and perfectly willing to let the time pass . . . detach
yourself from any feelings and thoughts about what is
happening . . . let your inner mind instruct your body
that there is nothing at all physically wrong with you . . .
all that has been happening is that your over-sensitive
nerves are playing tricks on you . . . and you are
misreading them . . . Just like sometimes excitement
can be mistaken for fear . . . so many other feelings can
be mistaken.

From now on . . . slowly and comfortably . . . you will
find you can venture out into the places that once
made you nervous . . . you find that each day that
passes you feel comfortable and more at ease . . .
very relaxed and calm in these places . . . You even
feel pleasantly excited . . . and look forward to
going out . . . the more you venture out the easier
it becomes . . . and the calmer you become . . . your
confidence grows and you feel so very proud of your
achievements.

You can go outside your house whenever you want
to . . . when you are outside you are calm, relaxed
and in control . . . your heartbeat is steady and your
breathing is regular . . . you are confident and happy
outside in the fresh air . . . you picture yourself going to
visit friends and enjoying their company.

Your home is a comfortable place to be . . . but you accept that you can go outside happily and confidently whenever you desire to do so . . . picture in your mind someone asking you if you are staying at home today and you say . . . 'No, I am going out' . . . you say this proudly and mean it.

You no longer focus on people's attention . . . if people seem to look at you it just won't bother you at all . . . it will seem just as if they are observing you with some slight interest . . . it will not bother you in the least . . . you have no need to feel self-conscious because you are so calm and relaxed . . . and whenever you need to do something quickly you find that is easy too . . . You take pleasure in observing other people and life in general . . . Now you find all you need to do to relax . . . take a deep breath . . . and allow that relaxation to soothe your body . . . and mind . . . allowing you to enjoy where you are . . . and deal with any obstacles that arise . . . Your mind clears and you find it easy to do all the simple things . . . that were once so easy . . . and have become easier again . . . You take control of any situation easily . . . whenever you need to . . . without a second thought . . . it comes so naturally . . . Very soon all the worries of the past will be in the past . . . and your future is bright and at the pace you feel comfortable with.

Fear of heights

As you relax deeper and deeper you find that the resources are within yourself to help you lose that old unwarranted fear of heights . . . Picture yourself climbing towards the top of a ladder . . . watch yourself shake with fear and see your fright . . . now allow yourself to see that the effects of fear can look very comical . . . Imagine a grown adult scared to death of a tiny spider . . . running away in a panic and squealing . . . Your fear is just as funny to a person who is not afraid of heights . . . You may have felt in the past that your fear is protective . . . but you know it to be destructive . . . now picture yourself in a real past situation when you were high up and it frightened you . . . imagine yourself reversing the process . . . like running a video backwards . . . to where you began before you were high up . . . Do this three times . . . and then rerun a new picture of yourself climbing up with ease and without any discomfort . . . See yourself happy and enjoying the experience . . . knowing that your natural protection is always there . . . you have just erased the unnatural protection . . . that has been causing you such distress in the past . . . no more . . . now life is much easier and your world is so much safer. Practise again with your ladder now, noticing that you can get higher easily . . . without fear . . . each time you practise in your imagination . . . you realize there is no fear left . . . and this is now your reality.

Public speaking

The fear of public speaking is one of the most common phobias people have and yet one of the least complicated to clear, as generally much of the fear has been created and reinforced by people being told it is difficult. It can affect people in many contexts, not least of all in the workplace. For this reason the script 'Fear of public speaking' can be found in Chapter 7 (*see page 115*).

Better networking

This script is for anyone who feels very uncomfortable at making friends at networking events.

Because you want to use your personality and persuasion that you use in your business and social life . . . with friends . . . you find that you become comfortable and confident at networking events that can bring you more business and contacts . . . Your good persuasive talk . . . that people like and find attractive in business . . . can now apply in your networking meetings . . . You find that when you are networking that you confidently give out your cards or brochures and look and feel confident and comfortable . . . instead of feeling shy and reserved you kick into the way you are with friends . . . you find a way of breaking the ice . . . You do this as you would in your business or with friends . . . you find the right conversation or questions to ask to put the person at ease . . . Like in business you may make mistakes

at first . . . but you soon learn what is good for you to break the ice . . . then you can talk easily to new contacts and do your business talk . . . Making use of networking . . . rather than being disappointed . . . and not enjoying it . . . and wanting to leave as soon as possible . . . instead a wonderful calmness and easiness and challenge replaces the negative feelings . . .
It becomes as natural as talking to your favourite friends . . . easy and natural . . . allowing you to enjoy networking events . . . in fact you look forward to them and to experimenting with your business talk and closing . . . Instead you enjoy the challenge.

Fear of crowds and people

Imagine you are speaking to one of your closest friends and feeling at ease with what you are saying . . . As you are talking a few people start to enter the room . . . It is a large room and there is plenty of space . . . You realize that this room is set out for a meeting, with plenty of chairs . . . and the people coming in are preparing to settle down on the chairs for a talk . . . Because you feel so relaxed . . . you realize that people strolling in are not bothering you at all . . . in fact, you feel more relaxed . . . knowing that the people coming in are friendly . . .

From now on you feel free . . . All the constrictions you have been aware of in the past disappear . . . and you can enjoy the pleasures of being in the outside world free from fear . . . It is not a dangerous place and all unnecessary fears will disappear . . . You can imagine them being put down a waste chute . . . thrown away in the rubbish bin or locked away in a trunk . . . or you can create a method yourself now . . .

[Pause for 30 seconds.]

You find that this new strategy clears your mind . . . so you are able to use your instincts . . . to protect you from people or places that would cause you distress.

The freedom from fear will release you . . . and enable you to enjoy places you go and people you meet . . . Your natural joy and sense of humour will replace your fears and you will automatically become more light-hearted and confident . . . This will attract people to you and you will make friends easily.

The following are suggestions to get you back into meeting people after you have done some of the phobia work immediately above.

Because you no longer fear the unknown . . . the benefits to your social . . . domestic . . . and work life are limitless . . . You are happier each day because you enjoy meeting people and being in their company . . . and you enjoy and look forward to being in new places and situations . . . new places excite you. With this new-found freedom you find that your personality is able to develop . . . exactly how you want it to be . . . You may want to be dynamic . . . you may want to be a good listener . . . you may want to be more up front . . . whatever you choose you find you attract and enjoy the company of the type of people you wish . . . who give you the friendship and companionship you are seeking.

You are happy in the knowledge that you have a more contented . . . exciting and dynamic lifestyle . . . as you find it more and more easy to go out and socialize with friends of both sexes.

The world is a happy, friendly and safe place to enjoy . . . a place to meet people and to achieve fulfilment . . . a place to enjoy a new-found confidence in yourself.

As you enjoy the company of your friends . . . they also enjoy your spontaneous and confident humour . . . You are realizing your full potential.

Resolving common fears

The next few scripts deal with the common fears of animals, spiders and snakes. For the animal one, you may want to insert the name of the specific animal or animals you feel phobic about.

Fear of animals

Imagine the animal standing behind the bars of a cage . . . just like at the zoo . . . imagine this vividly . . . now say the word 'relax' in your mind . . . breathe slowly and deeply . . . allowing your body and mind to relax . . . Now the animal is closer . . . less than a metre away . . . Now you are the animal . . . take the place of the animal . . . It is calm and relaxed in your company and you are just part of the scenery and it gets on with its life . . . knowing that you are not a threat or harmful . . .

and so it can relax and get on with its little life . . . As the animal, create an image of how the person ahead should behave . . . Now change places back and bring with you the information from the animal . . . now observe the information . . . consider it and realize how clever and sophisticated your answer is . . . You feel so relaxed now . . . knowing that you are able to live in your world with the species that once frightened you . . . You know you take sensible precautions when dealing with any animal or insect . . . But you know now there is no need for any unwarranted feelings except calm . . . and happiness.

Fear of spiders and creepy-crawlies

It's because you want to live your life to the full . . . getting the most out of every day . . . followed by nights of blissful sleep . . . that it is now time for you to take charge of your life.

It is time to drop the irrational behaviour that no longer serves you . . . there is no longer the need to be concerned about insects . . . no need for sleepless nights, no need to look silly and helpless.

Spiders and other crawling insects have all got one thing in common . . . they're all cold-blooded . . . that means, to them, you may seem a positive furnace! Certainly, with spiders we make their 'hairs' stand on end in fear . . . in truth, they are very frightened of us and, not being aggressive, they run as fast as they can to get away from us . . . when we chase them. They are so scared that they roll themselves into a ball and play dead . . . hoping we will move out of their now terrorized life . . . if they can avoid you they will . . . your world and their world exist side by side, but they want to have nothing to do with you . . . they just want to get on with their lives.

We know so little about their world . . . and if we did . . . we wouldn't fear them . . . many insects do really useful jobs for us, like eating woodworm . . . always remember that to them . . . we may even look like gods . . . compared to them we are huge . . . immense beings . . . to be avoided at all costs.

There is no need to kill them . . . because they cannot harm you . . . recognize the real situation . . . instead of your unreal fear . . . just let them be . . . going about their simple lives . . . or if the situation requires it . . . put a glass over them . . . gently slide some paper under the glass . . . taking care not to harm your small, wondering friend . . . then you can carry him to a place outside . . . your lives are separate again, as, indeed, your worlds will always be.

Remember that . . . FEAR . . . stands for Fantasies Envisaged As Real . . . negative fantasies are the source of all fears . . . 'being' in reality means that you cannot feel fear . . . you can only respond to a situation in an appropriate way.

You need never react in unnecessary phobic fear again . . . from now on you can respond as a conscious being . . . responsible . . . and completely in charge of the way you live your life . . . from now on, you choose your life . . . THIS IS FREEDOM . . . and it feels great!

Remember these are only some examples of scripts that I've used with clients over the years with great results. If you look on my website www.selfhypnosisthebook.com you'll find more suggestions that you can use as they are or personalize to your own liking. It is a good idea to reread Chapter 6 to remind yourself of the rules of formulating suggestions when personalizing them. It is easy to forget an important point that might make all the difference between a script that just works rather than one that will bring about great results.

RECAP

❖ The scripts have been tried and tested with clients and hypnotherapists for a number of years. With repeated listening, you will notice the subtle differences in your behaviour.

❖ If you read the scripts carefully you will get a feel for how important it is not to use ambiguous words or to make suggestions too complicated.

❖ Take note of the use of negative words in suggestions.

❖ If you want to stop smoking, the 'Stop Smoking in One Hour' script has been used unchanged since the 1990s with extraordinary results.

Conclusion

You now have all the tools you need to use self-hypnosis to improve any aspect of your life. However, with self-hypnosis you need to practise going into hypnosis and experiment with going into a deeper trance state. The more you practise, the easier it will be and the better the results. You can use the suggestions included in the previous chapters in order to become familiar with experiencing hypnosis and resolve any issues you may have. I would encourage you to experiment by creating your own tailor-made suggestions for your own circumstances. As with any new skill, practice makes perfect, but if you invest the time, self-hypnosis can be a life changer.

We all have busy lives and fitting a new activity into a full schedule can be challenging. However, putting time aside for a short, effective self-hypnosis session can reap numerous rewards both physically and psychologically. Even if you only use the Progressive Relaxation induction for stress relief, you will notice the difference. Less stress means better sleep, improved mental functioning, better relationships and the obvious physical benefits.

Some people listen to a relaxation or sleep suggestion just before bed: it calms the mind and takes care of thoughts that may interfere with you getting off to sleep. Generally, when you can't sleep it's because your mind is overloaded and simply does not stop focusing on everyday problems. Nowadays building this into your regular bedtime routine is much easier than before. You can have the recording to hand next to your bed and simply listen to it as you go to sleep. If you are in a quiet environment and won't be disturbed you don't even need headphones. You simply go to bed and listen and of course the recording will stop automatically. Before, it was very difficult to afford the equipment to record yourself clearly, as cheaper recorders had distracting noise and crackling in the background and even so, you would need headphones to get the desired effect.

For those intending to use self-hypnosis for business, I highly recommend reading Napoleon Hill's *Think and Grow Rich*. According to Don Green, the executive director of the Napoleon Hill Foundation, the book has been called the 'Granddaddy of all motivational literature'. It was the first book to ask boldly, 'What makes a winner?' The man who asked and listened for the answer, Napoleon Hill, is now counted in the top ranks of the world's winners himself. He is an excellent example of a person's perseverance, determination and having no limitations in his goals. If you make notes of key points when reading the book and include them in your suggestions you'll be programming your mind with knowledge gained from the world's most successful high achievers.

Having self-hypnosis on a mobile device means you can use self-hypnosis 'on the go'. Who wouldn't like a boost of confidence or a quick self-hypnosis relaxation session during a stressful day? If you're having last-minute nerves before a presentation you can listen to a quick 'Fear of public speaking' suggestion (*see page 115*) just before you go on stage. There are a multitude of situations where self-hypnosis can help us in our daily lives.

> *Once you've managed to include self-hypnosis in your regular routine you'll never look back. The results can be quite profound but ultimately it's up to YOU to use it.*

You may also find that, like many people who read about hypnosis, you simply want to know more about this intriguing subject: its history, its workings and more advanced techniques. And some people, as I have done, find hypnosis has been so beneficial that they want to help others.

When I became interested in hypnosis I was a journalist, and a skilled journalist is a fact-finder who doesn't waste time with misinformation. I applied the same skill to my thirst for knowledge about hypnosis. This was much easier in the 1980s, as it was far too expensive to self-publish books. I was lucky enough to interview some of the top experts in the field and they would suggest books I should be reading. So reading the credible books is the best way to go.

People often assume, incorrectly, that a hypnotist is a unique individual with a magnetic personality and, while

Self-hypnosis

this can be true, it certainly isn't the norm. In the past, hypnotists were portrayed as wide-eyed and staring at their 'victim' ready to put them under their spell. This is a cliché grown out of stage hypnosis posters and from people who didn't understand what hypnosis is. Old-style hypnotists wanted to maintain an air of mystery. The reality is somewhat different. Anyone can learn the skill and become a successful hypnotherapist and those who take my advanced hypnotherapy training courses come from a variety of professions; many have decided on a new career after reading one of my books.

If you do want to know more, to help you through your hypnosis journey, I have put together a recommended reading list which is an excellent guide to the books with the best information. You'll find more information about furthering your interest in hypnosis at www.selfhypnosisthebook.com and www.valerieaustin.com and in the resources section at the back of the book.

I wish you luck in your journey and hope that you find hypnosis as beneficial as my thousands of clients and I have.

References

1. Gauld, Alan, *The History of Hypnotism* (Cambridge University Press, 1992); 424

2. ibid; 89–101

3. Coué, Émile, *How to Practice Suggestion and Autosuggestion*, (1923, reprinted Martino Fine Books, 2010); preface

4. Kosslyn, S.M., *et al.* 'Hypnotic visual illusion alters color processing in the brain', *American Journal of Psychiatry*, 2000; 157(8):1279–84

5. Gauld, Alan, *The History of Hypnotism* (Cambridge University Press, 1992)

6. Forrest, Derek, *Hypnotism: A History* (Penguin Books, 2001)

7. Lang, Elvira V., *et al.* 'Adjunctive non-pharmacological analgesia for invasive medical procedures: a randomised trial', *The Lancet*, 2000; 355(9214): 1486–90

8. Blankfield, Robert P., 'Suggestion, relaxation, and hypnosis as adjuncts in the care of surgery patients: A review of the literature', *American Journal of Clinical Hypnosis*, 1991; 33: 172–86

9. Schwarzenegger, Arnold, 'Arnold classic', *MuscleMag*, July 1997

10. Loh, K.K. and Kanai, R. (2014), 'Higher Media Multi-Tasking Activity Is Associated with Smaller Grey-Matter Density in the Anterior Cingulate Cortex', *PLoS ONE*; 9 (9): e106698. doi: 10.1371/journal.pone.0106698

Bibliography

Bachner-Melman, Rachel, et al, 'Freud's Relevance to Hypnosis: A Reevaluation', *American Journal of Clinical Hypnosis*, 2001

Baudouin, Charles, *Suggestion and Autosuggestion* (Kessinger Publishing, LLC, 2003)

Coué, Émile, *My Method* (Doubleday, 1923)

Coué, Émile, *Self Mastery*, (George Allen & Unwin, 1959)

Crabtree, Adam, *From Mesmer to Freud* (Yale University Press, 1993)

Ellenbergen, Henri F., *The Discovery of the Unconscious* (Basic Books, 1981)

Elman, Dave, *Hypnotherapy* (Glendale Publishing, 1984)

Forrest, Derek, *Hypnotism: A History* (Penguin, 1999)

Fromm, Erika, and Kahn, Stephen, *Self-Hypnosis* (The Chicago Paradigms, 1990)

Fulder, Stephen, *The Handbook of Alternative and Complementary Medicine* (Oxford Medical Publications, 1996)

Gauld, Alan, *A History of Hypnotism* (Cambridge University Press, 1992)

Gibson, H. B., and Heap, M., *Hypnosis in Therapy* (Chichester: Lawrence Erlbaum Associates, 1991)

Gibson, Jack, *Relax and Live* (Moytura Press, 1992)

Hammond, D. Corydon, *Handbook of Hypnotic Suggestions and Metaphors* (Norton, W. W. & Company, Inc., 1990)

Hartland, J., *Medical and Dental Hypnosis* (Baillière Tindall, 1989)

Hayward, C., *What is Psychology?* (A.A. Knopf. Inc., 1923)

Hill, Napoleon, *The Magic Ladder to Success* (Penguin, 1930)

Hill, Napoleon, *The Science of Success* (Penguin, 2014)

Hill, Napoleon, *Think and Grow Rich* (Plume, 1937)

Jackson, Arthur, *Stress Control through Self-Hypnosis* (Piatkus Books, 1993)

Johns, Alfred E., *Scientific Autosuggesion* (Modern Coué Institute, 1947)

Kroger, William S., *Clinical and Experimental Hypnosis* (Pitman Medical Publishing, 1963)

Leslie, Mitch, 'Research Supports the Notion that Hypnosis can Transform Perception', Stanford Report, 6 September, 2000

Maltz, Maxwell, *Psycho-Cybernetics* (Pocket Books, 1960)

Ousby, William, *Self Hypnosis Through Scientific Self Suggestion* (Thorsons, 1996)

Playfair, Guy Lyon, *If This Be Magic* (White Crow Books, 2011)

Schwarzenegger, Arnold, *Total Recall* (Simon & Schuster, 2012)

Ward. Steve, 'Self-hypnosis Boosts Immune System', *Trends in Immunology*, 2001; 22(H12)

Watkins, John G., *Hypnotherapeutic Techniques* (Irving Publishers, 1987)

Weitzenhoffer, André Muller, *The Practice of Hypnotism* vols 1–2, (Wiley, 1989)

Resources

Books

I suggest you read these few books first, and if you want to study further please visit www.selfhypnosisthebook.com or www.valerieaustin.com for further information.

Coué, Émile, *My Method* (Doubleday, 1923)

Coué, Émile, *Self Mastery* (George Allen & Unwin, 1959)

Green, Don M., *Everything I Know About Success I Learned from Napoleon Hill* (McGraw-Hill, 2013)

Hill, Napoleon, *Think and Grow Rich* (Plume, 1937)

Johns, Alfred E., *Scientific Autosuggestion* (Modern Coué Institute, 1947)

Stone, W. Clement, *The Success System That Never Fails* (Pocket Books, 1980)

Watkins, John G., *Hypnotherapeutic Techniques* (Irving Publishers, 1987)

Also by Valerie Austin

Self Hypnosis (Thorsons, 1992, Harper Perennial, 2010)

Free Yourself From Fear (Thorsons, 1998)

Hypnosex (Thorsons, 1996)

Slim While You Sleep (Blake Publishing, 1994)

Stop Smoking in One Hour (Berita Publishing SDN.BHD, 1997, Blake Publishing, 2000)

. . . .

Reading a book is a great starting point for anyone interested in the subject of hypnosis, but if you want to extend your knowledge and gain practical skills there's no substitute for attending a training course with an expert and learning the skills in a hands-on practical environment. Here you'll find additional resources that may be useful to further your interest.

Workshops

You can gain a wealth of experience attending even a short training. Attending one of my two-day intensive Self-Hypnosis workshops will reinforce the basics you've learned in this book and develop your skills for using suggestions both for yourself and others. Other workshops available include 'Stress Management', 'Weight Loss' and 'Stop Smoking in One Hour' – the famous Harley Street smoking cessation technique for hypnotherapists. A brand new specialist workshop for helping cancer sufferers is also available. For hypnotherapists I have online training in Skypenosis and DVD training courses, as well as specialist courses on my yacht in central London.

Become a hypnotherapist

People from all different backgrounds gain an interest in hypnosis then decide to become hypnotherapists. My elite 7-day Advanced Hypnotherapy Diploma course teaches you everything you need to know to become a practising hypnotherapist. It includes techniques for personal and corporate clients, including how to deal with phobias, weight loss, age regression, marketing and speed-reading. The 'Stop Smoking in One Hour technique with the proven success rate is also included in the course. You can set up a business as a hypnotherapist confident that you have powerful techniques to change people's lives. Students also receive email support and the opportunity to attend individual and group workshops and online Skype training.

Mesmerism

Author, historian and hypnosis expert James Pool conducts Mesmerism workshops in which you can learn some basic techniques with hands-on coaching in using Mesmerism. As well as including a wealth of history and research on the subject, James imparts exclusive knowledge passed down to him from one of the last people to know Mesmer's secrets. The 12-month practitioner course provides a comprehensive and in-depth training in Mesmerism. Details are available at www.mesmerism.com

Retreats

If you prefer to 'get away from it all' when training, there is the option of attending a retreat in an exclusive environment designed to make your training experience in hypnosis or Mesmerism as relaxing and rewarding as possible. The idea came from 'Learning in Paradise' courses I ran on a beautiful tropical island in Malaysia, which proved to be extremely popular.

Hypnotherapy apps

You can download apps from iTunes containing the e-book and audiobook versions of my books *Free Yourself From Fear*, *Stop Smoking in One Hour*, *Self-Hypnosis* and *Hypnosex*. The apps also include free suggestion audios.

Specialist hypnotherapy packages

Specialist hypnotherapy packages are available if you want to lose weight, have a phobia or want to improve your relationship. These packages include a special audio recording and accompanying book focusing on each particular issue. Full details of the packages for 'Slim While You Sleep', 'Free Yourself From Fear' and 'Blueprint For Love' can be found on my website.

Personal Hypnotherapy Sessions

Austin Training maintains a register of Advanced Hypnotherapy specialists personally trained by Valerie Austin if you would like one-to-one therapy.

National Guild of Hypnotists

The NGH is one of the oldest and largest hypnosis organizations in the world and boasts a significant global membership of hypnotherapists and those interested in the field of hypnosis. For more information visit www.ngh.net.

For more information about training, products or one-to-one therapy visit www.valerieaustin.com or contact Valerie at valerieaustinhyp@aol.com or telephone +44 (0)207 702 4900.

ABOUT THE AUTHOR

Valerie Austin is a successful author, journalist, film producer and trainer with an international reputation in the field of hypnosis. A near-fatal car accident in 1978 left Valerie with amnesia, and after hypnotherapy enabled her to recover a big part of her memory, she was inspired to change her career from Hollywood reporter and magazine publisher, to train as a hypnotherapist.

Valerie went on to found her successful hypnotherapy training school, become a leading hypnotherapy trainer and publish five bestselling hypnosis books. She worked at the Priory Hospital in London as a consultant in hypnosis, specializing in food addiction and alcohol abuse. Her famous Harley Street Stop Smoking in One Hour technique has a 95 per cent success rate and is used by hypnotherapists worldwide. She has also used hypnosis in her corporate training courses to help CEOs and international business people maximize their potential.

Valerie is now training people to use self-hypnosis to help treat illnesses such as cancer, where sleep, pain, stress and self-worth are an important part of recovery. This research has brought her full circle, and she is now producing films and documentaries. Her latest film, *The Face of Cancer*, was screened at the Cannes Film Festival.

 valerieaustinhyp@aol.com   valerieaustinhyp

 hypnotherapytraining   @valerieaustin

www.selfhypnosisthebook.com
www.valerieaustin.com
www.austinhypnotherapytraining.com

Notes

Notes

HAY HOUSE BASICS
Online courses

If you're interested in finding out more about the topics that
matter most for improving your life, why not take a
Hay House Basics online course?

Each course is intended to provide a powerful introduction to a
core topic in the area of self-development or mind, body, spirit.
Presented by a renowned expert, each course includes:

**An overview of the topic,
including its application and benefits**

•

Video demonstrations of practical exercises

•

Meditations and visualizations to guide you

•

**Specially created text guides, available to
download for future reference**

Available at a special low price, these courses are
the ultimate route to a full spiritual life!

Find out more at **www.hayhousebasics.com**